"*Voyage of Purpose* is an exceptionally beautiful and well-written book. David's near-death experience is dramatic, and so is his cure from what should have been a fatal cancer. From such remarkable experiences, this book exudes an abundance of wisdom. This highly recommended book gives remarkable insights to help all of us along our own Voyage of Purpose."
—Dr. Jeffrey Long, radiation oncologist and nationally-recognized expert whose work has been featured in Newsweek, The Wall Street Journal, and Coast to Coast. Long has served on the board of directors of The International Association for Near-Death Studies and is actively involved in NDE research.

"*Voyage of Purpose* is an inspirational book that prompts one's curiosity, sense of validation, open-heartedness and peace of mind. Your soul will thank you for reading it."
—Kimberly Clark Sharp, MSW, LiCSW, author of *After the Light*, President, Seattle International Association for Near-Death Studies

"David Bennett is one of millions who have had a near-death experience; one of thousands who have written about it. You never get tired of these stories. Whether the individual was frightened or uplifted, there's something special about 'the telling of the tale.' David's *Voyage of Purpose* though, has a different ring to it. His is a raw and honest travelogue of a man who hardly had a chance as a child, then became a 'man's man' to make up the difference, took up diving, got caught in a storm that beat him up so bad he should have wound up in a coffin. In his near-death scenario he met his Soul Family, an experience that rocked him to his core. His life changed after that—new job, big move, later a divorce, remarried, then the discovery of massive tumors and a dissolving spine. What he went through to regain his health is the stuff of miracles; what he learned along the way is a message for all of us—about spirituality, about purpose, about the power of prayer and the reality of unconditional love. David is a gentle soul today, someone you want to be in the same room with, as just his presence heals and calms. In *Voyage of Purpose* he shares what he learns as he learns it. He takes you with him into the depths of spirit, so you can feel your own soul and discover your own truth."
—P. M. H. Atwater, L.H.D., author of *Near-Death Experiences: The Rest of the Story*

Voyage of Purpose

Spiritual Wisdom from Near-Death back to Life

Beth
thank you for
shining your light –
in your community!

♡
David
+
Cindy

David Bennett
& Cindy Griffith-Bennett

FINDHORN PRESS

Published in 2011 by Findhorn Press, Scotland

ISBN 978-1-84409-565-0

Edited by Michael Hawkins
Cover design by Richard Crookes
Interior design by Findhorn Press

Printed and bound in the USA

1 2 3 4 5 6 7 8 9 17 16 15 14 13 12 11

Published by
Findhorn Press
117-121 High Street,
Forres IV36 1AB,
Scotland, UK
t +44 (0)1309 690582
f +44 (0)131 777 2711
e info@findhornpress.com
www.findhornpress.com

Table of Contents

Acknowledgements

We would like to acknowledge and give a special thank you to the following people for their contributions, encouragement and support on the long voyage of writing this book:

Dan Chesbro and Carol Scoville for recommending I write down my experiences so long ago and pushing off this journey. We must, of course, thank Richard Hughson for being a quiet voice of acceptance that began true integration of these experiences into daily living; Pamela Liflander for believing in this book before we did, showing us the nuts and bolts that needed attention and helping to plot the course; Erin Clermont for editing and making the crossing so much smoother; Sabine Weeke, Michael Hawkins and all the people at Findhorn Press for giving us a home port.

We would like to thank those in spirit who continue to inspire, guide and encourage; Myrtle and Gleason Viers, Margaret Schiano, Tom Sawyer and Margaret Kean. Their voices may no longer be heard but their presence is strongly felt.

Finally, we want to thank our family and friends who are too numerous to list and gave so much encouragement and a few healthy shoves in the right direction. They filled our sails with love and energy that carried us through.

No duty is more urgent than that of returning thanks.
— *Saint Ambrose*

Cindy's Introduction

I first met David Bennett in Geneseo, New York, at a spiritual weekend retreat. Even then, he struck me as a quiet, observant, and gentle man. He wasn't as outgoing as others in our group, and I didn't think much about our meeting. About a year later, at another weekend retreat, we met again and it was clear that David had gone through a change. He was not just sitting back and observing—he was participating. I think that was the first time I really "saw" David.

What I saw was a shining light. David had a calming presence, yet his energy was invigorating. I now know that what I experienced was David with his heart open wide. It is intoxicating…and a little overwhelming, and you'd think, after being married to him for ten years, I would be used to it. But when he opens his heart and radiates that truth of his, I still have to catch my breath.

When I first got to know David, he wasn't talking about his near-death experience (NDE) as he does now. I knew he had an NDE, but I didn't know a lot of the details. Over the years, I have heard him share his story with hundreds of people and I learn something new each time. When he asked me to write his story, we didn't know where to start. We tried a few times, but we just couldn't pull it together.

In the spring of 2005, we were invited to visit Acadia National Park with part of the spiritual group from Geneseo. I had always been drawn to Acadia; I don't know why I was drawn. I just knew it was a place that I had to go. It did seem beautiful, yet it was more than that, but I had never gone.

We decided this would be the perfect opportunity. We brought the laptop with the idea that maybe we could gather our thoughts about the book during the 11-hour drive. Well, it's a good thing we could plug the computer into the car adapter. Something about David driving and me typing was magical. I still quite don't know who drove the car as David went deep into the light to recount his story. Luckily I type fast, because there was no stopping him. He talked and I typed the whole way—through New York, Massachusetts, New Hampshire, and finally across the border into Maine.

It was a special time in Arcadia. David climbed Cadillac Mountain and we were able to spend time with Tom Sawyer and some other dear friends. We were told that many musicians and philanthropists have found the beauty so amazing that they say it inspired them. Jim Chappell even chose Acadia for the name of an album he created after hiking the trails there. I think that it is a combination of the beauty, the sea and the energy of the place. It feels sacred. It goes deeper than just the beauty.

Acadia was the inspiration we needed, and the ride home was just as productive. The time flew by as I asked David questions and he went deeper and deeper into his experience. He even surprised himself, as details emerged that he had never thought about before. Someone must have been watching over us, because we arrived home safely and with his experience in the light down on paper.

After the trip, we kept the writing going during afternoons spent in front of the fireplace. David relived his time in the light over and over again while I recorded his experience in words. I took all the computer files with me on a trip to Australia and attempted to start writing the book. But I found it impossible to re-create the intensity of David's language. Every time I tried to capture his story in my words, I lost the connection to the light.

This was when I decided I must let the reader experience David's amazing journey the way I did, in his own words. It became clear this was the only way to share the full impact.

I feel incredibly blessed to be the one chosen to be his scribe. Every time I reread David's story, my heart opens a little more to the light and love he offers us.

I believe with all my heart that you will benefit from reading David's story as much as I did. Don't worry if you can only read just a little and then sit back and absorb it for a while. After all, it took a voyage of twenty years for David to be able to integrate his near-death experience and tell you his story. It is understandable that you might need a little time to integrate his incredible light and love into your own life's voyage.

— *Cindy Griffith-Bennett*

Chapter One

❧ THE EARLY YEARS ❧

No one saves us but ourselves, no one can and no one may.
We ourselves must walk the path but Buddhas clearly show the way.
— Gautama Buddha

In sharing my story I first want to introduce you to who I am. Not the statistics or events of my life that the public sees, but rather, the inner me, a spiritual connection to my true being. In order to accomplish this introduction we'll need to voyage back in time so you can have an understanding of why my life's course has changed its bearing so much. (And please excuse the nautical terms I cast about, because I am, after all, a sailor and engineer.)

I am telling this story for my own well-being and so others will benefit from reading it. My near-death experiences have changed my life, turning it upside down and inside out, and the effects from those experiences continue unfolding to this day—and will probably go on until I pass over once again.

I hope that by telling you my story of near-death experiences, you will see clearly all the changes it caused within my life and with my connection with Spirit. In doing that my goal is to help those who have had their own sort of spiritual transformative experience realize that change is inevitable and good. By reviewing our lives we can all have a better understanding of why everything happens as it does.

Before I relate this information about my early years it is important to understand that I do not view any of my past or present as good or bad. I view everything in my life as just the way it was, is, or will be. Eckhart Tolle expresses it so well in his book *A New Earth*:

> When we go into a forest that has not been interfered with by man,
> our thinking mind will see only disorder and chaos all around us.
> It won't even be able to differentiate between life (good) and death
> (bad) anymore since everywhere new life grows out of rotting and
> decaying matter. Only if we are still enough inside and the noise

of thinking subsides can we become aware that there is a hidden harmony here, a sacredness, a higher order in which everything has its perfect place and could not be other than what it is and the way it is.

Survival

We make progress in society only if we stop cursing and complaining about its shortcomings and have the courage to do something about them.

— *Elisabeth Kubler-Ross*

When looking back on my life it amazes me to see how my experiences prepared me for my death. One experience leads to the next, constantly preparing me for the upcoming challenges —very much like a new birth, you might say. Please do not view the extremes and swings of my life and death as good or bad. Instead think of them as a part of my wholeness or my true being.

As a child of a single mother in the late 1950s, I was bounced from family to family, never really belonging to one. It wasn't common or acceptable at that time to be a single mother. Some of the families I lived with had opposing and extreme religious beliefs that taught me to fear God and authority. In other homes I was subjected to foster siblings sexually abusing me. Bounced around like this I was always going to new schools. As the new kid in school in the Syracuse, New York suburbs, the class bullies usually singled me out as a target. Once, when I was in first grade, I was dragged off, beaten, and left lost in a swamp by some particularly tough older boys. I stayed in the swamp, wet, cold, and frightened the boys would return, until a neighbor found me wandering and helped me home well after dark. Thankfully, the foster dad of that home taught me how to use my fists with boxing gloves and a punching bag in the basement. That significantly reduced the number of lost battles later on in my youth.

In second grade, my plight came to the attention of a substitute teacher, Myrtle Viers. She and her husband, Gleason, who had no children of their own, took me in at the age of seven. Theirs was my first stable family environment. Even so, I had to walk to school and the bullies were again in full force. Knowing and becoming somewhat proficient in street fighting, I wasn't concerned as much about myself as I was for my new friends, who happened to be targets themselves. It was at this point in my life that I developed the ability to look ahead...as if I were floating above the rooftops. I could see where the bullies were hanging out, waiting for me. My friends and I could then avoid them by taking a different route to school. I didn't see anything odd in my ability. I thought everyone could leave their bodies and look ahead. But because I was not part of a "real" family, I thought my foster family just wasn't telling me that this was normal. And it followed that I wasn't going to let on to anyone that I could look ahead. I share this to show how isolated I felt at this early stage of my life. Because I didn't know how to have healthy relationships or interactions with others, I was already developing a need to be independent.

It was about this time that I started having recurring dreams. Three dreams stand out to this day. Each involves me dying. In the first and least frequent dream, I am a deckhand on a tall sailing ship. The ship is attacked and boarded. In the fight, I am killed. In the second, more frequent dream, I am walking along a path that borders a sheer rock wall. There is a landslide and I am killed instantly. The third dream, the most frequent, finds me working for a Spanish ranch that raises bulls for the bullfight arena. One of the bulls charges me while I am training it. The bull gores me, lifting me into the air and I am dead before my body lands. This dream would cause my body to lurch so violently that I was actually lifted a few inches (centimeters) off my mattress. In all of these vivid and violent dreams, I would awake, after experiencing my death, and find myself soaked with sweat and breathing heavily. People would tell me that you never die in your dreams, but that wasn't true for me—I died quite often in my dreams. Of course, I never said a word to anyone, keeping it all inside.

By the time I was twelve, I had this strong knowledge that I was going to die in my mid-twenties. I used to joke around with friends, saying, *"I'm going to live hard and fast because I'm going to die young."* I always visualized I was going to be stabbed just under my shoulder blade, into the lungs. I knew I was going to have incredible searing pain in my chest and die. Little did I know at the time how true this predictive knowing would become!

Meanwhile I was quickly learning how to be self-sufficient and manage on my own. If I wanted something for myself, like a new bike or jeans, I had to work for it. I shoveled driveways and mowed lawns to get what I needed. I saw my birth mother about two weekends a month if I was lucky. Mom-Marge was a fiery (dyed) redheaded party girl, and also a hardworking waitress and barmaid. Most of the time Mom was working when I came to visit. So if one of her drunken boyfriends wasn't at the apartment to babysit, I was brought to the bar or restaurant, where I became somewhat of a pet. When I was really little they would actually seat me on top of the bar. Again, this taught independence and how to make the best of a tough lifestyle.

When I was 14, Mom married James Schiano. I called him Jim or Jimmy because that's what the rest of his family called him. I was too old and had lived in too many homes to call him Dad. The crazy thing was, I was never told about their wedding. I found out much later that their "justice of the peace" wedding took place during a trip to Florida. Mom and Jimmy had a unique relationship—they loved to argue and pick on each other. It appeared more like screaming and yelling to most people, but somehow underneath all the demeaning they did truly love each other.

Mom and Jim never stayed in one place for long, and soon after they were married, they felt like it was time for a move. Tucson, Arizona, was their chosen destination and they decided they were going to take me with them. I didn't know it at the time, but Myrtle and Gleason were on the verge of adopting me to save me from this neglect and abuse. This was incredibly threatening to my mother. To Myrtle and Gleason's disappointment, we skipped town. That was the end of the Viers' short stabilizing influence. I didn't understand the pain my leaving caused the Viers family.

Arizona sounded cool to me, and I thought the move was a wonderful thing. I was only interested in what I could do in Arizona, the adventures I'd have as a 14-year-old. On the road, just south of Flagstaff, there was a lot of road construction and we had to pull our forty-foot (ten meters) house trailer through what looked like a goat trail for hours. After we cleared the construction and were on smooth road again, our trailer lost one of the driver-side tires. I watched from the backseat as the tire bounced down the road beside us. Now unstable, the trailer pushed our Chevy Suburban from one side of the highway to the other, spitting gravel in every direction. On one side of the road was a cliff and on the other a sizable embankment. Jimmy, who had been a truck driver, knew he had to get us safely off the hi-way so he pointed the truck toward the part of the embankment that leveled off with the pavement. He was only off by a little with his calculation because we left the road early, dropping down until the nose of the truck plowed into the next embankment.

I was in the rear bench seat and Schultz, our German shepherd, was chained in the back of the Chevy Suburban because he liked to lunge at other vehicles. Mom and Jimmy were in the front seat with Trixie, the little red Pomeranian. When we started swerving, I hung on for dear life. When the truck flew off the road, it bounced me high enough that I could look out the windshield. As we were about to meet the next embankment, I slammed hard back down on the seat. Schultz flew over me and the bench seat hitting Mom square in the back. Both dog and Mom slammed against the dashboard. Jimmy's head hit the windshield. The force of the impact was so great that the truck folded like an accordion, it pushed the front and back seat together and I was sandwiched between them.

The trailer jackknifed, and now lay on its side across the highway, blocking both directions. Drivers who witnessed the accident came running and helped us out of the Suburban. Mom was in unbelievable pain. Jimmy's face was covered with blood and glass. I was shaken, though, miraculously, did not have a scratch. The ambulance took us to the hospital in Cottonwood. I sat outside tending to Schultz and Trixie, listening to the quails whistle back and forth to each other. Not knowing the sound of a quail yet, I thought maybe someone over the ridge was whistling to us, trying to get our attention. Obviously I was in shock, and to this day I can't understand why no one thought to examine me. The dogs and I waited quite a while before a nurse came out to tell me that my parents were going to have to stay in the hospital. Jimmy had sent her out with his wallet and the nurse called me a cab. At fourteen I was left on my own with two dogs. No social worker, no nothing, just the clothes on my back. Luckily, the cab driver knew of some inexpensive rooms that were close enough for me to make the long walk to the hospital each day.

The lady who owned the rooms let me keep my canine charges as long as I kept them quiet and clean. She had heard about the accident from the cab driver, who had probably heard about it from the nurse. Good old small-town rumor communication. My two-room digs were just behind Main Street, on which a combination bar / pool hall / sweetshop / restaurant had a blue-plate special everyday for a buck! Of course the word got out about my situation, that I was on my own, and the waitresses made sure my plate was piled high. I can still remember those meals—that's where I learned I really liked chipped beef on toast. Usually the blue-plate was my meal for the day. I had to make Jimmy's cash last because I had no idea how long Mom and Jimmy would be in the hospital. Someone else helped me out with the dogs' food and my landlady loaned me plates and silverware. All I had to wear were the clothes I had on in the accident, and I washed them out in the sink every other night.

Every day I took the long walk up to the hospital in the Arizona sun to check in with my folks. I was too young to be allowed inside to see Mom in the women's ward, but the nurses let her know I had been there. The waiting area outside the women's ward was a scary place, having to hear women down the hall moaning or sometimes screaming. I detested sitting in the hospital. When Jimmy was able to walk again, he'd come out of his room and visit me in the waiting area. After about three weeks, Jimmy was discharged but Mom was there for another six months with a broken back. That three-week period in my young life taught me I could survive on my own, but its hardening effect sent me further into my own isolation.

We decided to stay in Cottonwood and the Verdi Valley. Mom changed as a result of that accident. She went from being a lighthearted party girl to being extremely negative toward everything in life. It didn't hurt Mom and Jim's love for arguing, though, which just got worse. I couldn't stand it, so I would spend as much time as possible away from home.

Mingus Union High School was up in Jerome on the side of Mingus Mountain. The school was made up of kids that were cowboys, Indians, Mexicans, or hippies. Suddenly there I was, plopped into the middle of all of this as a long-haired kid from New York State. The cowboys misinterpreted my long hair and thought at first I was a pacifist hippie kid. Boy, did they make a mistake. After I dusted a few of them off in the parking lot after school they left me alone, and they quit threatening to cut my hair. I fell in more with the Navajo, Hopi and Mexican kids. Their homes became my hideout. Their mothers and grandmothers saw my messed-up family life and kind of adopted me, sharing a lot of their beliefs with me. I found a sense of peace with these people, despite my negative family situation. When not hiking and exploring the deserts, canyons and mountains, I was listening to the grandmothers' stories.

Boys Wanting to Be Men

I have now understood that though it seems to men that they live by care for themselves, in truth it is love alone by which they live. He who has love, is in God, and God is in him, for God is love.

— *Tolstoy*

As you can probably sense by now I was a very brash young man who wanted to challenge everything—and even going so far as to put my life on the line purely for the thrill of adventure. I used to think of myself as an adrenaline junky. But most of the things my friends and I did were just the foolish undertakings of boys wanting to be men.

Like the time we heard that a friend's father had shot and stuffed a bear. Well, that was too much for our teenage imagination so two pals and I took off to hunt what the Native American mothers called the "grandfather bear" that lived in the mountains near our homes. So what that we had never hunted bear before—how hard could it be? With all our great years of wisdom we came up with a grand plan. Since I had the least amount of hunting experience and only a borrowed 30-30 rifle, I would walk through the center of the canyon where we had found signs of a bear and make a lot of noise. That way I'd herd the bear down the canyon. My companions would stay a little ahead of me, atop the canyon walls, and shoot the bear when they got a clear shot.

I could hardly wait for them to get into position so we could start our great hunt of grandfather bear. Once they did, I started moving up the canyon, yelling and beating the brush, which was great fun. I just knew that old bear would be running down the canyon in view of the sharpshooters at any moment.

I noticed my friend on the right falling behind me a little, so I shouted up at him to move faster. All he did was nod in recognition, which was just fine by me, because I was beginning to believe that maybe the bear wasn't even in this canyon. Nevertheless I kept waving for my friend to keep moving and he kept waving for me to do the same. I didn't get why he had to tell me that. But I instantly forgot about him when, from behind, I heard the deepest grunt of my life. The hair on the back of my neck vibrated. I cautiously looked over my left shoulder and saw that big, very big, old bear swaying back and forth, and looking at ME. I didn't waste another second. I turned and ran. I didn't stop running until I reached the end of the canyon, where I sat down, my back to a tree.

When my friends caught up with me I had cooled down enough to threaten them with slow torture for not warning me, even though they claimed they were trying to tell me. By the time we got home we had convinced ourselves that we were great bear hunters and that the bear was lucky to have so narrowly escaped us. Funny thing, we never went bear hunting again. We never told our parents, or even the neighbor I borrowed the rifle from, about our great hunt.

We boys who wanted to be men were taught respect and honor for the strength of the Creator that day. Unfortunately, the lesson wasn't brought home to our hearts so we could live it in our lives. We continued to tempt fate in our further adventures with this knowledge in a slumbering state inside us.

Two years after arriving in Arizona, Mom and Jimmy wanted to move back east to Syracuse. I guess the grass was always greener someplace else for them. Once again I had carved out a life for myself only to have it ripped away. Back in Syracuse, I took a course on scuba diving at the YMCA. It was then that I fell in love with diving. Who knew that this new passion would eventually lead to my death?

Learning to Play the Game

Whatever games are played with us, we must play no games with ourselves, but deal in our privacy with the last honesty and truth.
— *Ralph Waldo Emerson*

I had gotten a little of Arizona and the Verde River in my bloodstream, so as soon as I graduated high school, I moved back to Arizona and that Valley. But times had gotten tough in Arizona and good-paying jobs were scarce for a young man. I realized I needed more education. My interest in diving and the water had not diminished, and I rather liked the idea of becoming a US Navy diver (I couldn't be a Navy Seal because my vision wasn't good enough). The Navy recruiter informed me that with my high aptitude scores if I went to the Navy's engineering school and become an engineer, I could then go to the Navy dive school. This all sounded grand, so I did basic training in San Diego, and then attended engineering school in Great Lakes, Illinois. I did well in both and received some meritorious advancement.

Soon after I was assigned to my first ship, the chief engineer called me to his stateroom with other men from my division. Everyone else in the meeting was a petty officer or higher in rank. He told us we were the core group of the engineering division. I kept to the back of the room because I figured I must have come at the wrong time to the wrong meeting. I was relieved when the meeting was over and we were dismissed. After that meeting Lt. Commander John Stepien started coming to our engineering space looking for me, and when he found me he would be incredibly critical and demeaning. I learned to hate him.

I'm a survivor and I learned Stepien's game pretty swiftly. So he'd have nothing to be critical about, I got very good at my job. To do that I not only had to learn my job, I had to learn everyone else's job as well. I qualified for all the watch stations in Main Control, Engine Room #1. This served me well, and I started advancing in rank. At this point, our ship received orders to Guantanamo Bay for war exercises. When we were at battle stations, my role was to stand next to Lt. Commander Stepien, and relay all the communications from the four engineering spaces to him. He would then respond with the orders needed for the battle conditions and I would relay these orders and queries back and forth to the four engineering spaces. It sounds very confusing, and it was at first. But I found I could fragment my thought processes so I could listen to the communication man in each of the boiler and engine rooms, relay the information to the Lt. Commander, then relay his instructions back and keep it all accurate.

During one mock battle scenario our engine room was hit. The petty officer in charge froze and didn't know what to do next. Because I had trained in all the jobs within our engine room I stepped in and successfully finished the scenario. The observers who graded the exercise couldn't penalize us because we took all the correct action, even though the petty officer froze. The next day the petty officer was transferred out into Repair Division and I was promoted to his position. I was only a second-class petty officer, but I was in charge of Main Control, Engine Room #1. I never found out why Lt. Commander Stepien singled me out, but I now have the highest respect for the man. I'm thankful he pushed me so hard.

While I was in charge of the engine room, a young man was put under my command who was clearly unstable. I thought the best course of action was to try to understand and get to know him. In talking with him, I realized that his life growing up was amazingly similar to mine. Instead of choosing to be self-sufficient as I did, however, he chose to be a victim. He allowed himself very little self-worth or self-esteem. I tried to help him as much as I could, but in the end he tried to commit suicide and was removed from the ship. He acted as a mirror for me, showing how the way we perceive our life experiences and the choices we make are critical to how we develop. At that time if someone was psychologically messed up everyone wanted to put the blame on his upbringing—it was the parent's fault. I never believed that line of reasoning; we all make choices, even as youngsters, when responding to challenges.

I find this philosophy is similar to the *I Ching* #29, one of the oldest divination systems of the Chinese classic texts, also known as the Book of Changes—*An empowered person observes how water changes its shape to fill any space it encounters, and learns a lesson about survival, success, flexibility and consistency.*

We all have the choice to see our experiences in life as opportunities for growth or reasons not to move forward. Flexibility comes when you learn to go with the flow or system you find yourself in. The Navy taught me how to play the game and be successful.

At the end of my four years I chose not to reenlist and become a Navy diver but instead use the GI Bill to attend a commercial dive school and become a professional diver. I could become a diver faster that way, so it was worth it to give up the reenlistment bonus in exchange for bigger salaries in the future. I was first in my class at dive school. That, along with my Navy engineering training, helped me land the job of Chief Engineer on the research vessel *Aloha,* owned by International Underwater Contractors (IUC), the same company that owned and ran my dive school.

Now in my mid twenties, I had been having a long-distance relationship since the end of my Navy days with a woman back in upstate New York. We got married, and shortly after that I transferred to California where I continued to work on the research vessel. It wasn't long before I moved my new wife to the tiny apartment in Santa Barbara, California. I was out to sea for eight to nine months out of the year doing my dream job: diving and working on the ship. Although it probably was not the best way to start a new relationship, we made a go of it.

So in conclusion over the early years of my life, I had learned to work hard in order to survive and be successful, but many tried to take advantage of me. Some of them were good friends, family members, or business partners who saw an opportunity to take something. Every time this happened it whittled away my trust in others and something inside me grew hard and cold.

The first twenty-seven years of my life taught me to go after what I wanted. Adversity was my teacher and it made me stronger. I had to fight my way through life, and thus my philosophy was simple: *"Cut your swath through life and sur-*

vive. "Something else that kept ringing in my head was advice from my stepfather, Jimmy, who would always tell me, *"Don't tell nobody your business."*

So I kept to myself and held my cards close to my vest. I knew what I wanted out of life and I went after it. I soon forgot the simpler days of Arizona. Those two credos and my fighting spirit served me well…that is, until March 1983.

Chapter Two

❀ THE OCEAN OF LIGHT ❀

As the rivers flowing east and west
Merge in the sea and become one with it,
Forgetting they were ever separate rivers,
So do all creatures lose their separateness
When they merge at last into pure Being.
— *Chandogya Upanishad*

One night early in March 1983, I was working as the chief engineer on the research vessel *Aloha*. We had just spent the day evaluating a new remote-operated submarine or submersible as we called them in the industry, with the manufacturer's representative. He was a strong-minded ex-marine who wanted to beat the storm coming our way and get to the airport and his flight home.

The seas were rough as we attempted to enter our homeport of Ventura, California. The harbormaster radioed the captain that if we entered the harbor the ship would probably bottom out if a wave broke under her hull. Even on a good day the harbor entrance was shallow for our large ship, and this was by no means a good day—the storm was moving in even faster than we expected. We watched from the ship's bridge a few miles offshore and decided to wait and bring the ship into the harbor after the storm broke, hopefully, sometime the next day.

Besides the manufacturer's rep., several crewmembers were anxious to get home, so the captain decided they could leave the ship on a smaller boat. Our giant research vessel's daily costs were incredibly high, especially when we were out at sea and not on a job, so to keep costs down it was a reasonable choice to send home some crew members who were not needed to bring the ship in. If it had been a calm night one of the deck crew would normally take clients back to shore, but in weather this rough the captain directed the chief engineer to accompany the returning group as well. The plan was for me to bring these folks into port, and then return to the *Aloha* for the overnight.

As we prepared to leave, we saw some large swells, but we couldn't see any of the surf zone, which was miles away. That sort of thing doesn't show up on your radar. We all knew this was going to be a rough ride in, and figured that even though all the members of the party were experienced divers and submarine operators we'd better break out the life vests just to be safe. We had to scramble around the boatswain's locker to find the old life vests. These canvas-covered, fiber-filled vests, the kind they used in World War II, looked as if they had been through a war or two. They were so filthy they had to be beaten and brushed clean before we could put them on. Most of us had not worn a vest in many years. Grudgingly, I put on the grimy Mae West that was handed to me.

We checked our position on the radar one last time, plotted a course to the harbor, and loaded up everyone's gear. Normally we would have taken the 18-foot,(4.50 meters) open-bowed runabout *Liberty* to shore, but tonight we loaded the Zodiac, a vulcanized rubber boat that we used to retrieve submersibles. It could handle much rougher seas than the *Liberty*. Even though it sat very low, the Zodiac had a V-4 engine and could really fly across the water. It was an extremely dark night with fast-moving clouds, and one of the crewmembers had wisely brought a flashlight so our little boat could be seen.

The captain turned the *Aloha* abreast to the wind and waves to make it easier to deploy the Zodiac. The ship created a calm area for lowering the Zodiac into the ocean. Once aboard, the deckhand took the center steering console to drive the boat and I took the bow to navigate. Normally I drove the small boats but I chose to let the deckhand drive that night. I felt I knew the harbor better and I could see more from the bow. Our low position in a small boat amid the large swells and troughs made it very difficult to see the lights of the harbor. When we were in a trough we couldn't see the shoreline. It was only when we were on the crest of a swell that we could glimpse the faint harbor lights. I stood on the bow, hanging on to the bowline to steady myself, and tried to locate the harbor buoys, which were being bounced around, most of the time hidden inside a trough or behind a swell.

The captain had left the ship's deck lights on, but we soon lost sight of the *Aloha*. We kept trying to ride the crest of a swell to get our bearings and then move forward through the trough. But the more we moved toward shore the deeper the troughs became. The wind whipped the tops of the waves into a constant horizontal spray of salt water in our faces. We didn't know it then, but we had been driven a mile south of the harbor by the wind and waves.

The Wave

Have you not read of: "Know ye not, that ye must be born of water and of the Spirit?" The water in material the mother of life; the Spirit the Father, or the moving to bring life. Is it possible, then, that a man when he is old, shall again enter his Mother's womb and be born again? Ye must be born of water and blood. Blood, a manifestation of force that through which life manifests in its various forms. Water, the cleansing force as one moves from experience to experience.

— Edgar Cayce

We could hear waves crashing, which meant we must be getting closer to shore. Instead we were two miles offshore, hovering over a sandbar that was creating the crashing waves. A wave broke beneath us, and suddenly we were falling. Everyone hung on and luckily we were able to stay in the boat as we slid down that wave for 25 feet (6.25 meters). I shouted over the roar of the waves for the deckhand to turn the boat around and head back out to sea where it was safer. The mate quickly responded, but the sky had gone black where the clouds should have been. All I could see was a ridge of white foam above our heads, which caused me to shout, *"Oh Shit, This Is It!"* as the wave crashed down on us in a split second. The wave packed an incredible amount of force, folding the boat in half like a peanut butter sandwich. Some of the men were trapped inside the fractured Zodiac. Three of the four inflatable pontoons were ruptured when the aluminum and fiberglass floor disintegrated. The motor snapped right off the transom.

Catapulted from the bow into the ocean, I was tumbled around in the water as the wave crashed down on me. It was the most raging violent force that had ever attacked my body. While wave after wave crashed over me I lost all sense of direction as the ocean tossed me around like a doll. When I opened my eyes and blew some bubbles to get an idea which way was up, the sand and salt burned my eyes. But it was so black I couldn't see the bubbles anyway. I did not know which way was up.

My years of experience as a diver had taught me not to panic, because if you panic you will surely die. I'd learned that a strange thing happened to me in dangerous situations. A clear calm sense comes over me, allowing me to work through the danger. So I knew not to try to swim for the surface because I could be swimming the wrong way. I could tell by the pressure in my ears that I was in deep water, past the sandbar. My lungs burned. I longed to take a breath of new air as the furious sea kept tossing me around. I was getting cold, very cold. I hoped for the old life vest I was wearing to carry me to the surface, but the surface did not come.

As a trained diver, I knew how to hold my breath for quite a while. I could tell my brain was starving for oxygen as a feeling of euphoria came over me. In dive school, I had been forced to experience oxygen deprivation in a safe and controlled environment. The instructor slowly decreases the oxygen going into your dive helmet so that as you breathe, you build up carbon dioxide. The instructor also cuts off your air while you're on a dive so that you can experience that sensation. During these training sessions, you have to run a dialogue with the surface through the communication device in your helmet, explaining what is happening to you and how you are feeling. This further helps you remember the effects of oxygen deprivation. So though I was remembering everything I learned, trying to keep calm and hold my breath, I began to realize I might die. I started to have some regrets as my life's earthly concerns flashed into my mind: *"Is my life insurance paid up?"* and *"Will my wife be taken care of when I am gone?"*

I couldn't hold my breath any longer, and I couldn't find my way to the surface. I tried to breathe the salt water. I clearly remember the burning, choking and pain in my lungs as I breathed in the saltwater and went through the agony of dying. The agony quickly melted away into darkness.

Quiet of the Void

The simple, absolute, and unchangeable mysteries of heavenly Truth lie hidden in the dazzling obscurity of the secret Silence, outshining all brilliance with the intensity of their darkness.

— *Dionysius*

I wasn't afraid. It was more like feeling surprised by the total darkness and the shocking absence of noise. The sea had dissolved from violent roaring to a complete absence of sound. I was no longer aware of the deluge. It wasn't as if I had gone deaf; it was more like the booming percussion of the waves didn't exist where I now found myself. I was in a void and I couldn't sense my body. It wasn't an out-of-body experience, in which I was able to observe my body; rather I was in absolute blackness without my physical body.

I can see how this might be frightening for some people, but because what had preceded this state—my last experience in life—was violent drowning, this actually felt calm, quiet and peaceful. In the Pacific Ocean, the currents from the north keep the water very cold. I knew my body should be experiencing the frigid March water temperatures. Yet, I was actually starting to feel warmth, as if my consciousness was wrapped in a thick blanket. It gave me a sensation of total tranquility.

It didn't feel as though I had been there for a long time, but I was curious, thinking, *"Where am I?"* I had not yet come to the realization that I had died. Instead I wondered if this was yet another stage in the euphoria, or something more I had not experienced it in my training. It was not.

The darkness was emptiness, not good or bad. It was lacking emotion. But I was comfortable, no longer in pain. I was totally alone. By the time I'd reached this rich black void, I had given up any regrets and stopped thinking about my life, dying, and loved ones left behind. It was only me in this blackness. I was focused only on myself, which was so opposite to my normal approach in life.

I began to sense a connectedness to this void. The fertile blackness seemed infinite. Yet there was something more, something supportive, and I had a knowing that the state I was in was the most natural thing in the world. I started to feel comforting joy and happiness. Although I could not quite grasp the meaning of this perception, I sensed there was more going on around me. I sensed something bigger, larger than myself, *more* than myself. I felt as if I should be communicating with this darkness. There was an omnipresent intelligence at hand, and somehow I knew I should move on. The feelings of being supported and joyous kept growing.

An Ocean of Light

Read not the Times. Read the Eternities. Conventionalities are at length as bad as impurities. Even the facts of science may dust the mind by their dryness, unless they are in a sense effaced each morning, or rather rendered fertile by the dews of fresh and living truth. Knowledge does not come to us by details, but in flashes of light from heaven.

— Henry David Thoreau

Slowly, ever so slowly, light started to appear within the darkness. A dim glow was growing lighter around me and I could see a brighter light off in the distance. Everything was growing brighter. It was as if I was surrounded by this light, wrapped in it. At the same time I felt as if I were getting closer to the brighter light in the distance. It wasn't clear to me if I was moving toward the brighter light in the distance or it was moving toward me. It was not a tunnel. The light was in one specific place and it was getting brighter and brighter: a steady stream of brilliant light. As I got closer I started feeling the light. I felt welcomed and loved. As the light got brighter, my feelings intensified. I was being lifted up emotionally as well as moving toward the light and as it got brighter I felt as if it were enveloping me, taking me into what I could only call Love. I was becoming a part of its Love.

The Light was brighter than any light I had ever experienced. As a chief engineer on a ship, I had many occasions to use an arc welder. The light emitted from the arc is so bright that you have to wear protective eye gear in order to look at it without burning your eyes. The light was brighter than that, yet I could still view it comfortably. I could see more clearly in this light than I could in life. Since childhood, I've worn prescription eyeglasses; in this light, no correction was necessary. I could see distance and detail in a way that had never been possible with my own mortal eyes. The light was the most beautiful vision you can imagine.

I found myself moving at the fringes of this brilliant light, continually drawn toward a denser area within it. I could not help myself. It seemed the most natural thing to do and yet it also felt especially familiar. I was happy and filled with joy. I felt so comfortable and loved. Slowly I began to realize I didn't have a body. I was a single fragment of this light. I was trying to look down. This seemed funny and odd to do because I didn't have a head or eyes, so it is not as if I actually looked down. My vision worked in any direction I chose; I didn't have to physically move to see in any direction. My physical body was gone; I was becoming formless, a sliver of light, which was like the light around me. As the intensity of the light around me increased, the intensity of my fragment of light increased, and I began to merge with it.

I didn't judge this transformation. I just accepted it. I was in awe of this change I was undergoing, and my instinct told me that this is what was supposed to happen. I have to say it was a pretty smooth ride. The love was incredibly empowering—it was a part of everything and everything was a part of the love.

The light was mostly white, but it had segments of blue and gold. The light seemed to be composed of billions upon billions of light fragments that pulsed and breathed. The light was constantly in motion even thought I remained stationary.

Every time I explain my experience in the light I can feel the touch of the Love that accompanied it. It is still incredibly emotional for me even many years later. In the light, without a body, I could handle that level of love because I had left the physical side of emotion behind. It is not that you don't experience emotion when in the light. But in the physical body, you have a physical reaction. In our physical body we feel excitement in our stomach and love can make us light headed. In the light I felt love, joy, passion, and excitement without the physical sensations. I had no physical reaction that might cause one to say, *"This is something I want to distance myself from," "I am not ready"* or *"I am not worthy."* I was simply accepting and awed.

Not only was I in awe of the Love, I also had a greater understanding and knowledge of life's mysteries. The universe suddenly made sense to me. If I pointed my thoughts in a certain direction, I was faced with the answers. They were all available for the asking. Even more amazing, I could see and think about more than one thing at a time. This wasn't the same as when your brain moves from one thought to the next. Instead, the information came from all directions—instantly. I had no trouble comprehending everything simultaneously.

The light was alive with consciousness, as if the souls for all living things past, present, and future were interconnected, sharing and shining their Love. It danced and pulsed with their lights to combine into one spectacular illumination of Love and Knowledge.

Meeting the Soul Family

A family is a place where minds come in contact with one another. If these minds love one another the home will be as beautiful as a flower garden.

— Buddha

Three light fragments were becoming brighter, breaking away and moving toward me. They were not clearly defined but silhouetted. I recognized these shapes as other beings. As they grew closer, I could sense them projecting thoughts of *"Welcome Home,"* as if we were family and there was immense joy in our reunion. I immediately knew who these beings were. I recognized their energy and I could sense their individuality through what appeared to be their warm, deep and expressive eyes. I never had strong family feelings in life. I did not have strong family ties and connections. Although I had brief periods in my life where I felt connected to a family, it was nothing like my ties to these beings. This felt stronger and more binding than anything I had ever experienced in my life.

They were so excited to be there with me and to see me home again. I cannot express strongly enough how much they felt like family to me. I just knew unequivocally that I was home, and it felt so exceptionally magnificent. They were supporting me and helping me by projecting waves of love and compassion. I was overcome with the joy of feeling I finally belonged somewhere.

More light beings were coming and joining us. They didn't communicate, at least not in a way you and I are accustomed to. Their form of communication involved projecting a knowing and comforting energy that contained more information in a millisecond than our mortal thoughts could assemble in a day. A dozen members in all joined our circle. Some of them were behind others, so I couldn't distinguish them as clearly as the beings closest to me, but they were all around me. They all felt like family, but not as close as the first three. I was now truly home, together with my family. Since then, I have come to call them my Soul Family.

The Life Review

It is a light which issues forth to do service under the guidance of the Spirit. The Divine Light permeates the soul, and lifts it above the turmoil of temporal things to rest in God. The soul cannot progress except with the light which God has given it as a nuptial gift; love works the likeness of God into the soul.

— *Meister Eckhart*

My Soul Family conveyed a message to me that we were all going to move to another area. They didn't communicate this in words, though I immediately understood. We traveled into another area of the Light that was like a sphere, a translucent globe. Once this sphere was completely around us, I started to experience my life. It was as if I were looking at it from inside out, living my life through other people's perspectives and simultaneously reliving it through my own perspective. This view was astonishing and wonderful. And the depth of this life review was more than all-encompassing. It was…ineffable.

The life review moved along more or less chronologically. I could see the effects and consequences of my original actions and/or reactions spread beyond the area of the sphere, like ripples in a pond. Not only were there images to see, but I also experienced feelings of others and how my actions in this life had touched them. I could feel their joy, happiness, heartaches, disappointments, and love—all their emotions in regard to my actions. I was aware also of my Soul Family's excitement and exhilaration to be here experiencing this along with me.

I have difficulty explaining the intensity and speed of the life review because everything was flowing continuously. Some parts had a larger significance, and there were parts of my life review that I'd have preferred my Soul Family not to see. I didn't want to have to admit things that I had done. To become the chief engineer in my twenties I had to step on a few toes. If someone didn't agree with my point of view, I would walk right over that person. I was ashamed that my newfound family had to experience those times in my life. Amazingly, they didn't judge me by my experiences, not even the events I was not proud of. They were merely observers, experiencing my life with me. They didn't hold any judgment pro or con. They seemed to relish my experiences.

Beyond my Soul Family's support, I was also aware of the Consciousness of the Light. When I think of God today, it is as a Consciousness of Light, with billions and billions of souls attached to that consciousness. The Light seemed to be observing, acting as a supportive and an incredibly loving constant during my death.

During the life review, along with not having a sense of my physical body, I existed in the Light without the drama of my life wrapped around me. All the fictions I had created in my life of who I thought I should be were stripped away, because the Consciousness of Light knew me better than I knew myself. I experienced my true self—what I now call my True Being. I felt as though this review of my life was meant to help me grow and evolve. Surprisingly, some of the smaller incidents in my life took on a greater importance during the life review. At the time these incidents were forgettable, hardly noteworthy. But once I saw the aftereffects, especially how my actions affected others, I became aware of the bigger picture. In our lives we are always thinking about leaving a mark and trying to make our lives matter. The accomplishments you think are important, like building something that will exist beyond you, or getting a job promotion, aren't necessarily the things that are going to be the most important in your life review.

For example, while living in Arizona as a young man, I had a job in a small town called Clarkdale, apprenticing as a butcher at Fairway Foods, the local department/grocery store. The store had an old-fashioned butcher counter, where we would weigh and wrap each item. One day an older lady came into the market. I recognized her because she came in frequently, and everyone who worked in the market would cringe when they saw her and scatter, trying to avoid her. She was so negative and cranky that no one wanted to be around her. And every time she came in, she would stop by the meat counter.

At first I felt the same way about this lady as everyone else. Then I decided to make up a game. I was going to try extra hard to get her to smile. It wasn't easy and it took quite a few months, but I never gave up. In fact, I began to enjoy the opportunities to treat her nicely. Then one day she came in after having bought a special roast I'd prepared for her. She started to tell me how much she liked that little roast…and that was when it happened. Her cranky old face just melted into the biggest smile you'd ever want to see.

Soon after on her visits to the market she wasn't as cranky as she used to be. Over time, she actually became one of my best customers and I looked forward to her visits. In life, I only recognized my part of the experience with her. However, in my life review, I saw how the other employees felt about this lady, and how their attitudes changed as she softened over time. I also got to experience her emotions, her joy in finding acceptance in that one little chore of shopping in the market.

This small event had more significance in my life review than many of the major accomplishments I'd prided myself on. I learned that it is more important to live your life day by day, and do the best you can. Cherish your experiences, good and bad, big and small. Try to be as helpful, compassionate and loving as you can. Living life in a loving manner generates the most powerful impact in the life review. Those actions create the largest waves of positive aftereffects.

At this point the experiences and feelings changed in my life review. I was being shown images that were not from the life I had just left. I had no references to them, which really confused and disoriented me. I was having direct interactions with people I didn't recognize. I was in locations I had never been. Yet these foreign experiences were just as vibrantly real and intense as those I recognized in my life review. My Soul Family continued supporting me, buoying me up during this, not with words, but with thoughts of immeasurable love and compassion.

Then I heard a clear, distinct voice that didn't emanate from my group. I sensed it came from the Light itself. I completely focused on this voice. I stopped paying attention to my experiences that were going on in the sphere and the group. I listened carefully to an incredibly loving voice, which told me, **"This Is Not Your Time, You Have To Return."**

When I heard that message, my first response was *"Oh no, I want to stay right here! I like it here, just where I am. I've found love and a family I never knew existed, I do not want to go back and continue living a physical life."* I resisted, pleading, arguing against agreeing to the request. Then I heard the voice again. This time the Light said, **"You Have To Return, You Have A PURPOSE."**

The word *purpose* kept echoing in my true being, resonating throughout my Soul Family and me. When I heard the second phrase, it was so loving yet so forceful that I could not argue with it. I couldn't argue because I understood the truth within it. When you are a part of the Consciousness of Light, you are a part of the all-knowing, which is enormously humbling. Suddenly, I understood that I had to return to my body and continue living my life: I knew that this was what was meant to be. I also understood the 'whys', although I cannot remember that part now and wish I could. I just knew I might not want to do it, yet clearly I could not argue with what was supposed to be. The Light was like a parent who is so full of love that I had no other choice but to agree.

Although we were still in the sphere, the experiences of the life review totally faded away. Up until the second I accepted the fact that I had to return to my body, all of my Soul Group stayed with me. After my acceptance, all but the original three merged back into the Light.

Back to My Body

The willow which bends to the tempest, often escapes better than the oak which resists it; and so in great calamities, it sometimes happens that light and frivolous spirits recover their elasticity and presence of mind sooner than those of a loftier character.

— *Sir Walter Scott*

I was back in the ocean. I instantaneously became aware of my body, though regarded it still as something separate from myself. Lifeless and suspended in the water, it was still being tumbled and blasted by sand and sea. I watched it without emotion, already longing to return to the Light. I did not want to return to my body, which appeared like a confining, heavy sack of flesh, not at all attractive. My being was feeling so much larger than my body, freer and complete. Returning meant losing my sense of connectedness. Separating from the Light and rejoining my body was the hardest thing I had ever been asked to do. It was more painful than drowning.

My body was in a very bad breaker zone, being buffeted and beaten by the waves as it rolled around under the sea. The sea state that night was estimated somewhere between 25 and 30 feet (6 to 6.5 meters). The storm was so incredibly rough that on shore it caused a nice sloping sandy beach to erode into a 13-foot cliff (4meters). The lines from the Zodiac were flailing around the boat's wreckage, floating loose. Now, a sailor knows how to care for his lines. One of the things he will do to protect lines from fraying is to weave the ends back into the line itself with a knot called an end splice. If a line has one end attached to a boat with the other end free, the free end is called the "bitter end."

The Zodiac was an inflatable boat with four pontoons filled with air. All but one of the pontoons had burst. Somehow my arm, in all that violence, had become tangled up in the one pontoon that still had air. The bitter end of the bowline was hitting my chest over and over. When the next set of waves hit, the rope dislocated my shoulder and thumb as it pulled my body to the surface.

I watched with my Soul Family, who were observing, as another set of waves slammed my body against the pontoon. Finally the waves hit my body against the pontoon with so much force that some of the water was pushed out of my lungs. Simultaneously, my Family gave me a shove. I experienced a rushing, buzzing vibration, and then I was back in my body. As I was entering my body my Soul Family projected the knowing that they would always be around me. Instinctively, I inhaled my first breath of air in a very long time.

My Soul Family was visibly gone, and now my lungs and eyes were on fire and my head was pounding. My body felt dense, as if it was frozen lead. If I were not tangled up in the wreckage I would have immediately slipped beneath the surface again. I coughed, threw up, and tried to breathe again. The cold waves kept pounding me. I still kept being pulled down. My first conscious thought after returning to life was "*Why do I have to live this life?*"

At the same time, an understanding nagged at me that I needed to survive. Resonating within me was the question: "Purpose, Purpose, Purpose? What Purpose? I have a Purpose?" I only knew I needed to survive because of that word. I knew there was some *purpose* to my being alive, living my life.

Chapter Three

❁ THREE GIFTS ❁

*Men go abroad to wonder at the heights of mountains, at the huge
waves of the sea, at the long courses of the rivers, at the vast compass
of the ocean, at the circular motions of the stars, and they pass by
themselves without wondering.*

— *Saint Augustine*

I was absorbed about my purpose and the need to survive. In the distance, I
could barely hear my name being shouted over the roaring sea. My shipmates
were looking for me. Somehow, they had made it to the surface safely. In all this
chaos, one of them had actually hung on to the flashlight and they had gathered
around it. They had already figured out who was missing, and now they were
looking for me. I tried to call out to them, but I was still coughing up seawater,
and my lungs were on fire, so my reply came out more like a squawk.

They finally spotted me floundering in the wreckage and fought their way over
to me. By now the storm had pushed us a little toward the shore, but we were still
at least a mile (1.5 km) off the coast. We all hung on to the fragment of our boat
and began to kick-swim toward the dim glow of the shoreline. The swells were so
forceful that we'd all have to put up an incredible fight if we were to make it in.

Although somewhat untangled from the lines, I was still having trouble staying above the surface. I kicked off my boots, thinking that their steel toes were the
problem. I clearly remember saying to myself, *"Damn, there goes ninety bucks for
that new pair of Redwings!"* Of course, losing the shoes didn't help. I kept slipping
below the roiling surface and grabbing the lines to keep my head above the water.

While I was fighting for my life, I was undergoing changes as a result of my
experience with the Light. These changes were making themselves known. After
I returned form the light there was still a connection to that incredible knowing
of things beyond our normal perception, which is part of the Light Consciousness. This gift made me realize that something was wrong with my life vest. As
I mentioned earlier, experienced divers and seamen under normal circumstances

never wear life vests. It was only because of the extremely rough weather that we grabbed these grubby vests. Mine was so old that the canvas lining had shredded in the course of being thrashed by the sea and the fiber filling had become saturated with seawater. The Coast Guard has since banned this type of flotation device, exactly for this reason. My vest, full of water, was acting as an anchor, dragging me down. I tore off the vest and it immediately sank, never to be seen again!

That little event with the vest, within this night of so many horrendous events, stuck in my mind for days following. An object that was supposed to save me actually drowned me, only to be saved by the 'bitter end'. I know I would not have had the strength to fight much longer if the Light had not let me know about the problem with the vest. Clearly, I was not meant to die on this night.

Once I could stay above the surface, it was easier for me to keep my good hand on the Zodiac. I could then kick-swim and do my part to help cover the mile between the shoreline and us. As we got closer we had to cross through another surf zone, where we tried to ride the waves into the shore. When the initial wave hit the Zodiac, the force snapped her transom in half. The transom with the outboard engine went to the bottom, or so we thought. Once we reached the second surf zone we found the engine dangling beneath us, attached by a chain to the bottom of what was left of the boat. The engine and chain turned into an anchor until the next powerful wave lifted us up and pushed us in a little farther. Finally, one of the divers, Bill, picked up the outboard engine on his shoulders and walked it in.

Once we reached land, one of my mates popped my dislocated shoulder back into the socket by placing one of his feet on my neck and the other under my arm, then pulling steadily on my arm. I lay there in the sand for quite a while feeling the earth beneath me. My battered body was still numb even though we were out of the frigid waters. Eventually, I beat my thumb against my hip until it too went into alignment.

We had all survived. Everyone was struck by how close we had come to death, but we didn't say a word to each other about the accident or our incredibly long time in the water. We knew how close we had come to not making it back. For most young men, bravado takes over after a close call—we boast of all the brave things we did to save ourselves. Or we laugh at the events to relieve some of the stress. I know, because I'd reacted that way after being in tight spots before. None of that happened on this night. Instead we were quiet and introspective, a good indicator we were exhausted and still in a state of shock.

I was lucky enough to still have my keys clipped to my belt loop, so we decided to find our way back to my van. Four of us lifted the broken shards of the Zodiac and started to carry the wreckage toward the marina and my parked van.

Bill again picked up the engine and led the way with a bleeding foot, which got cut on some glass on the beach. I guess I wasn't the only one to kick off my boots. None of us were familiar with this strip of beach so we headed inland where we thought the coastal road should be. We came upon a pickup with a couple inside. It must have scared the daylights out of them to see five bedraggled sand-coated men come out of the raging sea to ask them for a ride to the marina parking lot.

After we loaded everything into my van, we stopped by another shipmate's house and notified the captain by ship-to-shore operator that we would not be returning the Zodiac tonight. Then I drove everyone home from Ventura Harbor to Santa Barbara. Yes, as nuts as it sounds, I drove and there was not a word said by anyone all the way. I just did it. All the way home I kept thinking of my time in the Love, the Light and with my Soul Family.

Home Sweet Home

If you want a happy family, if you want a holy family, give your hearts to love.

— *Mother Teresa*

By the time I reached home, it was well toward morning. I stood barefoot outside my apartment door, afraid to go in because I was covered with sand from head to toe. The only clothing I had left was my jeans with mini-sandbags for pockets. I started to strip off my pants outside the door of our apartment. Suzanne, my wife, was awake because, although I didn't know it yet, she'd had a nightmare in which I died. This had so frightened her she couldn't return to sleep. When she heard me outside the door she thought it was an intruder so she peeked through the peephole and saw me undressing. Of course she had no idea why, so she yanked me inside.

I wasn't thinking very clearly. I was fearful that I was going to come into the house, make a mess with all this sand, and upset my wife. She was shocked and relieved to see me, though I wasn't scheduled to be home for another day and that worried her. The minute she touched me, she could feel how ice-cold my body was. Then she saw how I was covered in sand. Even my eyes and ears were full of it. I told her that we had an accident bringing some of the men into the harbor.

Trained as a nurse, her first act was to warm me, to get my body temperature back up. She pulled and prodded, trying to get me into the bathroom. I was more than willing to take a nice warm bath but I was moving very slowly. In the safety of our apartment, I had mentally retreated inward, reviewing the events of the night. First she first put me in a cool bath, I didn't even notice it wasn't warm, and she slowly increased the water temperature. After a moment, I thought she was trying to scald me and I came back to the present. I didn't realize that my body was still hypothermic. Lucky for me Suzanne knew what to do. Eventually, I began to feel a little inner warmth. She checked with me to see if I had broken anything. I had already forgotten about the shoulder and thumb. They were totally numb, just like the rest of my body, and seemed unimportant anyway.

She was trying to question me, get a reaction. I wasn't responsive because I couldn't stop thinking about my experience. Eventually I said, *"Hon, I think I died tonight."* This confession so frightened her that she started slapping me. Afterward, she told me that she hit me because she thought I was in shock—I wasn't answering her questions. All I knew was that she didn't want to hear about me dying, which I could understand. It sounded crazy to me, too. I decided then and there that I wasn't going to talk about it. I was not going to share my experience with her or anyone. How could I tell my shipmates? I couldn't. We trusted each other with our lives, but the topic of death was unthinkable and taboo.

I see now how Suzanne's reactions were based on the fear of her dream earlier that night, and that she was only reacting instinctually. I wish I had known then that others had gone through this experience, and that fear was a common response from loved ones when they tried to talk about it. If I'd known, maybe I would have been more comfortable telling my wife about the Light, would have tried to dispel her fears. I had not an inkling how to express what had happened that night. I had no words to explain the grandness and the intensity of the Love. I thought I was the only person who had ever experienced anything like it. If I had known what I know now, known more about NDEs (Near Death Experiences), I could have communicated with others, read books or contacted a support group in my community. The Internet was not available in 1983, so there was no place to easily research a subject or find support. If I had known more about NDEs I would have tried to work it out and dispel her fears. I'm glad there are more options available today.

It was close to dawn before my body returned to normal temperature and Suzanne helped me into bed.

Seeing With New Eyes

If you realize the self in your inmost consciousness, it will appear in its purity. This is the womb of wonder, which is not the realm of those who live only by reason.

— *Diamond Sutra*

My rest consisted of catnaps. I literally crawled out of bed a few hours later. The numbness was wearing off and my body started to feel the pain. I felt like I had been run over by a bus, a very big bus. I could have stayed immobile in that bed for a week, but I couldn't stay in that small apartment. There is a freedom in the Light, and now, back in my body, I felt restricted and limited. All the while I was awake lying there I was being drawn outside. I needed to be outdoors, where I would not feel so confined. The urge was relentless—I needed birds, palm trees, plants and rocks. I hobbled out to our apartment complex's landscaped gardens. I had never noticed how beautiful they were.

I could see the life energy in my surroundings. There was an aura of light around all of the plants and rocks in the planting beds. I could feel and touch them without physically touching them with my hands. My engineer brain kept trying to figure it out. How is this possible? I could hear rhythms, notes, a lyrical kind of energy when I really focused. It was not like a song. I was sensing more than hearing physically, the sound wasn't always clear. If I had to relate the sound to something, it would be like the subtle fairy tingling sound you read about in children's books. Not knowing about auras, I didn't have words for it. It was all a new kind of energy—glowing life forces in everything. The palm trees were the most majestic experience. I could not get enough satisfaction looking at trees. Actually, I was in awe of every living thing including the groundcover and rocks. It was all so alive.

The closest I came afterward to these experiences was in a sweat lodge, where you pray intensely to Spirit in combination with the physical exertion of sweating in the extreme heat. This creates a level of exhaustion that allows you to be more open to perceiving life energies that we normally just don't see. Within your exhaustion your body/mind relaxes so you can be in your spiritual center seeing energies that are there all the time.

This new way of sensing life forces made me examine all of what was going on around me. As an engineer, I needed to figure this out. *"Why suddenly had life changed?" "How come I can now see this?" "How is it possible that I can see and hear what I could never sense before?"* After my garden walk I was still certainly hurting. The walk had not loosened my beaten body at all. I was bruised from head to toe, yet that didn't stop the strong urge to go back to the ocean. I called Bill, a dive crew supervisor who was in the accident with us. He, his girlfriend, Suzanne and I went down to the ocean on the premise that we were going to salvage debris from the *Zodiac* that might have washed ashore in the storm. Even though the storm had pretty much subsided, the ocean was still violently crashing about. The 25-foot-plus (6 plus- meters) waves had eroded much of the smooth sand beach; it was now re-placed by a 13-foot (4meters) cliff. We were shocked that we had been in that storm. Now, in the daylight, I could see with my physical vision the tremendous fury that had been going on out at sea the night before. But now, I could also sense a larger picture of Earth energies—the rhythmic patterns of the waves with the tides and the moon. The sea was such a great place to experience this. I could see Earth as a living, breathing planet…and I don't think I'd given that much thought before. During my youth in Arizona, some of the Native American grandmothers had shared stories with me about Mother Earth. I didn't really take their lessons seriously about how the Earth grows, expands, and contracts. They'd say, *"She is breathing"* Now after my time in the Consciousness of the Light I could understand their meaning. You can bet I did not breathe a word of this to my friend Bill.

Instinctively, I knew what I had experienced the previous night was something difficult for anyone to understand. Let alone me. Me…try to understand? That was a laugh! I was an old salt, and up until now I'd kept my feet firmly on the ground or on the deck of the ship. I was an engineer who only saw things in black and white. And after my wife's reaction I was afraid to talk about what I had experienced; I was afraid Bill and my co-workers would think I was totally nuts. I didn't know about Dr. Raymond Moody's books or any of the research into near-death experiences that had been going on since 1975. I spent most of my life at sea, so I missed a lot of what was going on in our culture. This new way of living, of being able to sense life energy, had left me dazed. I think the group on the beach that day saw me as spacey, but they didn't know one-tenth of the extent of my inner turmoil.

I also didn't want to say anything because no one else seemed to notice my new perspective. If I talked about it, they would think maybe I'd gotten a severe crack on the head in the storm that had made me a bit crazed. Heck, I honestly thought I was going crazy, and I certainly had no intention of telling anyone that. I had to find a way to deal with this. No one talks to the Light of God, especially not me. Only old priests, monks, or nuns can get that close. I wanted my old life back, but that was not going to happen.

That first day back from death was incredibly complicated. I was moving at less than half speed compared to when I was in the Light. My new appreciation for life was so much bigger than I was. Part of me was still connected to the Light, and that was freaking me out as well. So I did what I thought was best, which was to focus on the moment. Doing that I was able to get through the first three days of living in a new reality and processing this radical shift in my life.

Acceptance

Everything harmonizes with me, which is harmonious to thee, O Universe.
Nothing for me is too early or too late, which is in due time for thee.
— *Marcus Aurelius*

Now remember, I had been the guy who cut a swath through life in order to survive. That was my philosophy. Having an experience in the Light was a gift all by itself, but exposure to the Light of Consciousness leaves one with new clear perceptions or gifts. After my near death, I was given what I call my three gifts: *Acceptance, Tolerance, and Truth.* They seem like very simple concepts, but they can take lifetimes to really understand let alone master. As I have come to understand them they have become my shinning beacons. The first gift I dealt with was Acceptance.

Before my near death, or as I came to call it my 'new life experience', I had no idea of acceptance. I had spent my teenage years going to school and hanging out with friends or working. My family life was dysfunctional, so I spent most of my time trying to escape. My friend's grandmothers would tell me the stories of Great Spirit. I felt I knew all about this Spirit thing, but in reality all I knew were the stories. The stories spoke of how we were supposed to live our lives, but I had been walking through life dreaming of how I was supposed to be, not truly accepting who I was.

After my new life experience, I gained a new understanding of acceptance. During my life review I faced how my human side and my spirit nature worked together. Most of the time they didn't work together because I did not yet understand the connection. With the benefit of the Light Consciousness I got to watch all the repercussions of my actions, and how they affected others. I suddenly learned how my life could touch others without my knowing it. I now knew that I am in the perfect place at all times and should be experiencing the present moment. By experiencing my life review with love and non-judgment, I knew who I was. I could accept that I had faults and strengths. By recognizing this I could start to work on myself to make myself a better human. I no longer needed to beat myself up over my failures. Instead I could learn from a mistake, accept it and move on.

What I am trying to say is, I didn't know who I was at twenty-seven years old. I had cloaked myself in a false sense of who I thought I should be, a macho diver/ ship's engineer who could fix or rig anything. Acceptance was a seed that was planted in me during my near-death. I didn't come to full realization right away, but I got a glimpse of understanding.

The grandmothers' taught me to live the natural way in tune with the earth, walking in a respectful manner. I now wanted to reexamine and investigate that natural way of living. I wanted to walk my talk with this new acceptance of who I was. I could move forward in my life and, I hoped, come to terms with my new reality and spirituality.

Tolerance

My heart, if you want to sit by a thorn,
what can I do?
If you do not want to pick flowers
what can I do?
If you do not see His beauty
iIlluminating the world,
what can I do?

— Rumi

Immediately apparent during the first three days of living in my new reality was the concept of tolerance. Tolerance allows you to see that others have their own goals and their own paths. I learned not to take on other people's burdens, or at the least, understand that other people's burdens are not necessarily always a part of my personal path.

There are times in our lives when we do pick up other people's burdens. An example is dedicating time in your life to serve in the Peace Corps., to work for our environment, or to help a close friend or family member through a rough time. I am not saying that you totally divorce yourself from another's suffering, you can remain compassionate, but you understand that you don't need to own it yourself.

Wow, this tolerance thing was all new to me. My previous form of survival tactics had nothing to do with being tolerant of others. I thought it was normal to try to change others. Like a spouse might do, trying to change his partner into something he wants or needs. That type of behavior shows a complete lack of tolerance, even if you feel it is for a good purpose, aim, or goal. In this physical life we are unable to see the big interconnected picture of the universe, so how can we know what is good for another individual. I was still able to choose whether a person's actions were something I wanted to be around, but that involved changing me, not the other person.

Suddenly I had a way of recognizing and respecting the beliefs and practices of others. From watching my own life review, I recognized that everyone is in their perfect place as well and experiencing what their life's path navigates for growth.

Prior to this new insight, if someone argued with me, and I didn't agree with his or her argument, I would discount it totally. I definitely would not try to understand that person or their opinion. Now I see that there is always another side. Thank goodness I was given this gift of Tolerance. It meant I did not have to own other people's opinions when they were in disagreement with my point of view. That allowed me to not discount the opinions of other souls.

If I took in everyone's opinions, I would be frozen, unable to move any direction because I would have all these opposing views inside. Tolerance was such a foreign thing to me because I had never given anyone else's opinion any consideration. To the old me nothing existed outside of my self-involved world. Most of that was a product of my early choices in life, but now I found myself with an opportunity to change that. It was an amazing realization: I could be accepting and tolerant of someone's path without feeling I was condoning it. Even conflicting views didn't threaten me anymore, and I found myself able to distance myself when necessary.

We should be in awe of all life. Unconditional love for all beings brings a reverence for all life and removes the want for others to be something they are not. Simply observe nature, each being doing their part for the greater whole. This brings peace within and a sense of our individual place in the world.

Truth

Turn not to the outside world! Into thine own self go back!
In the inner man alone resides truth.

— *Saint Augustine*

Tolerance led me to my third gift; Truth. Even as a small child, I had a sense of when I was going against my true nature, or if I behaved in a way that I thought would be more acceptable to the people around me. I knew that was not who I truly was. This self-created fiction slowly became me, even though it was false. Over time I became lost in the false self I had constructed. The love from the light and the Consciousness of the Light showed me my true self, without the fiction. The Light knew me better than I knew myself—or gave myself credit for.

It is difficult to shed a false persona overnight. I kept trying to wear the old me after the NDE, but it didn't fit anymore. It took me a few years to accept my true self, as I had experienced it in the Light. Now, when I am working with my true self, I call it my Truth.

There are many ways to express truth, but before my experience the only truth I knew was factual truth, which comes out of a book. Personal truth is more abstract than factual truth, often felt through experiences and even representing an understanding beyond ourselves. Truth is a root to our personal philosophy of life.

When you do something just because it makes you feel happy or you get that feeling of *"Aha! This makes sense to me or I understand this,"* it usually has to do with your life philosophy and your personal truth. Your personal truth can vary 180 degrees from another person's. Once we have learned Tolerance, however, we can allow that and it can be okay.

People can observe the same event and because everyone sees that occurrence from different angles and points of view, we all come away from that event with a different understanding. In life that is how our personal truth works.

Because it feels good when we experience our truth, we don't want to change it. We want to hang on to it and not let it go. The funny thing is that the harder we hang on, the more it slips away from us. After my near-death experience, I had quite a few go-rounds of trying to understand my truth and my philosophy because it kept changing as I kept growing. And boy was I growing fast.

As I grew, I was becoming a more accepting and tolerant individual, but I also tried to hang on to what I had known as my personal truth. Then I would realize that my truth had changed because I had changed my philosophy, even if just a fraction. Your truth fluctuates with your growth and direction of your life path. I don't believe that life's path is a straight road. I believe it takes lots of twists and turns along the way. In effect our personal truth becomes a moving target. And if you think about it, a winding road can be a fun road to travel.

I now understand that mine is a fluid truth. It comes from my heart. When I weigh my experiences against the truth in my heart instead of my mind, I can move forward in my life much more quickly. Living a life that is more true brings great joy, an indescribable joy, because you start pursuing all those things that make your heart sing. For example, finding your creative side can jump-start learning where your truth lies. When your heart sings, you know you've touched Truth.

After the three days of feeling present yet also in the Light, I had my new tools of Acceptance, Tolerance and Truth. I knew I had to try to live a more loving and compassionate life. My battle cry became. . *Acceptance, Tolerance and Truth*. I took some time to reflect upon what the grandmothers had taught me and dived deeper into Native American culture, attending seminars, powwows, and reading books. It was the start of looking deeper into my spirituality in general.

Half Here—Half There

Yesterday is but a dream, tomorrow but a vision. But today well lived makes every yesterday a dream of happiness, and every tomorrow a vision of hope. Look well, therefore, to this day.

— *Sanskrit Proverb*

I took away from the NDE only what I felt I could handle and was comfortable with. I had taken such a hard look at myself that I knew some of the problems and issues I had to work on. But knowing my issues didn't mean I was going to change overnight. I still had the same temper and people still pushed my buttons the same way they did a week earlier. But now I was *aware* of my emotions, thoughts, and reactions. I was confident that over time I could change them.

I believe that a near-death experience makes us look at who we are in a way that most people never have a chance to. You see all of the good and the bad of the past. You understand that this is where you are right now, but that doesn't mean it is where you have to stay. Our future is full of opportunities and potential for positive change.

My near-death experience left me in a state of shock for those first three days. Not a physical shock, more like a spiritual shock. Let me explain: After returning from the Light, it stays with you for a while. I've met other experiencers since who have expressed the same feelings after their return. Being in the light made me feel as if I was in God's hands, and I did not feel worthy of that blessing—*Who am I to have experienced that level of love? I wasn't very spiritual before my death!*

When I was in the presence of Grace, the love I felt was for everything and everyone. There is a feeling of oneness within the light, which, once I came back, was difficult to live without. During the next three days I still felt like I was in God's presence. It was too overwhelming for me to deal with—I was walking around half there and half here. At the same time, I was living with my heart wide open, and if you have not experienced that, I'll tell you that it is very emotional and painful. Plus, I had an incredible longing to go back into the Light and stay there. I tried to forget it. I tried to not think about it any way I could. I put my focus on the next job I had lined up in an effort to get my thoughts back to living my life and getting the experience behind me.

I could barely deal with the extrasensory awareness. I wanted my subconscious to take the enormity of experiencing the light and the love and package it up nice and tight and store it away. I didn't want to feel the separation and loss of my Soul Family. Eventually, I was successful and my NDE was wrapped up and placed on the highest shelf in my subconscious mind with a big sign that said Do Not Touch, so I knew not to go there.

During that three-day period I attempted to get my life back and move forward. After all, I am a survivor. I was more than slightly relieved when my new-found ability to view life energies diminished because it was one less distraction and one less reminder of the NDE. So I kept my three gifts and tried to move on, even with that nagging sense of *purpose.*

The storm was never spoken about again at home and none of us spoke of it at work. Working in a rough, gruff male environment where tempting death was a source of pride left no room for that. I think all of the crew respected the fact that any one of us could have died that night—and I sure wasn't going to tell them I had! I now had to find a way to integrate my near death back into this life.

Longing to Return

To wake at dawn with a winged heart and give thanks for another day of loving; To rest at the noon hour and meditate love's ecstasy; to return home at eventide with gratitude; And then to sleep with a prayer for the beloved in your heart and a song of praise upon your lips.

— *Kahlil Gibran*

Over the years I've said hundreds of times, *"Dying is hard, but returning to life is even more difficult."* Once you have experienced the Light of God, the Peace, the Love, and then have to return to a confining, restrictive, and unknowing physical body, you long to go back to love, knowledge, and freedom. It is not that I would ever do anything to shorten my current life. I came back understanding the preciousness of life's voyage, high or low. It is a privilege to have this life, and I want to squeeze out every drop of experience while I am still here. But that intent doesn't stop the *longing* to return to the Light. The longing to return home, to my true home, is with me even to this day. It has become a part of who I am. I know now that I need to experience all this life has to offer and bring it home with me when this life ends. That purpose still rings in my being.

Experiencers are reminded of the Light's Grace on a daily basis. Every time my NDE comes to mind, or I touch it in any way, I am reminded about how wondrous and free I was while in the light and connected to the unlimited consciousness. I use my experience as a gauge in making every day judgments and decisions. While searching for my purpose I came across the Tao Te Ching and verse 50 sang out to me.

> *But I have heard that he who is skillful in managing the life entrusted to him for a time travels on the land without having to shun rhinoceros or tiger, and enters a host without having to avoid buff coat or sharp weapon. The rhinoceros finds no place in him into which to thrust its horn, nor the tiger a place in which to fix its claws, nor the weapon a place to admit its point.*
>
> *And for what reason? Because there is in him no place of death.*
>
> — *Lao-tzu*

Lao-tzu is speaking about the way we face our mortality and live our life without the fear of death. When Death calls on me once more, I will go happily unless Spirit tells me not to cross the threshold. Death no longer holds any fear inside me because I am happy to enjoy what life sends me. Further on in this book you will read about another opportunity I had to return to my home in the Light. But Spirit reminded me of my purpose and I did not cross the threshold. Fear of death and the suffering that fear causes, could not sink its claws into me due to my knowledge that we do not die. I have witnessed my essence and experienced the end without ending, and now at this moment I am sure of life and there is no place of death within me.

Chapter Four

❊ TEN YEARS OF CONCEALMENT ❊

This Self is never born, nor does It die, nor after once having been, does It go into non-being. This Self is unborn, eternal, changeless, ancient. It is never destroyed even when the body is destroyed.
— *Bhagavad Gita*

Because I believe the longing to return is a natural aftereffect of a near-death experience, I will not make it a focal point of this book. I believe you have to acknowledge it if the longing is present, however. Acknowledging it is healthy and allows you to move forward.

Questions haunted me immediately after my return: *"Why did I have to come back?" "Why did I have to go into the Light?"* These questions are all related, and most can be summed up as: *"Why me?"* I do not profess to have the answers. Everyone's life path is different, and who am I to say that someone is not supposed to go through, say, an obsessive phase after returning from a spiritual transformation. Although focusing on one aspect of life or death is not a way to live your life in balance. Obsession can be a hard thing to back away from—it takes on its own self-perpetuating energy and can become our new God to follow. Our minds are very good at making things grander than they need be, leading us toward our obsessions. For example, if I were so wrapped up in my longing to return to the Light that I dedicated my whole life to finding ways to be a Light being again, I would miss many opportunities to live this life and be who I am. I would be trying to make myself into something I am not meant to be in this lifetime, or I might judge myself as not being capable of achieving that goal. I would waste this life, my purpose unfulfilled. I have accepted my return to life and am happy living my life knowing that when my time comes to return to the Light it will be a joyful reunion.

Once my feeling of being half in the Light subsided, I knew I had to find a way to go on living this life. The course I chose to do that was to work on myself. Was that the easiest choice? Maybe, maybe not. Nonetheless, the love and lack of judgment in my near-death experience made me want to look for belief systems that followed similar paths. When I was outdoors, in nature, I felt a love that seemed unconditional, freer than what I encountered in my personal or public relationships, so I started looking for belief systems that honored nature. It wasn't long before I was brought back full circle, to Arizona and to my encounter with the grandmothers' teachings when I was only a teenager. It reminds me of my first attempts to go inward to find relief and insights.

The grandmothers spoke to me often about sacred silence. They instructed me to find silence within myself, and that the best way to do it was on my own. So one day, 14 and alone, I climbed one of the foothills near my home. When I reached the top I found a level plateau that was quiet and undisturbed by our small community below. It was a spot where if I sat back a little from the edge, I could overlook the entire valley and not be observed.

I immediately felt a connection to my new hideaway, so close and yet so remote, a perfect place to spend time in search of my sacred silence. I was nervous at first because I had to do this alone and my imagination was creating unrealistic images. My teenage mind was dreaming up all sorts of magical places of fantasy. I felt as though my mind had become my enemy. Thoughts and doubts interrupted my early attempts, and I began to think the sacred silence was an old Indian fairy tale. Nevertheless, I still enjoyed my time of solitude on the plateau. It was better than listening to my stepfather and mother bicker. I was able to relax and think clearer than any other time or place. If that was all that happened then it was a positive use of time.

Sometimes I would let the calm warm feeling of the sun on my skin be the only thing on my mind. I created my own ceremonies to quiet my mind, such as drumming or listening to the wind talk. Then, one hot, dry afternoon, I witnessed a strong wind stir up a sandstorm on the other side of the valley. I kept watching the spot, mesmerized, as the sand was lifted into the air making larger and larger clouds. The sky and air were soon a yellowish color, and the sandstorm reached halfway across the valley, racing toward me. The sun was almost covered, and I could smell the change in the wind, how the sand was mixing with the wind, making it thick and earthy. As I stared into the storm my body went numb, I felt myself falling, half flying, down to an unknown landscape below. I landed softly on a small hilltop and unexpectedly there, slightly behind me and to my left, was an elderly Indian. He began to speak to me warmly, telling me that this was our sacred place. I was frightened at first by the incredible power I sensed in the old man. He told me the fear was my own, and that I had brought it with me. The power was also mine, and I only had to return to this place, inside myself, to use it.

We sat quietly together while he gave me some of this strength. When finished I then found myself sitting at my plateau hideaway again. The sandstorm had passed. Blinking away the sand and dirt in my eyes, I dusted myself off, exhilarated. I had found it! After all this time the sacred silence had come to me.

After that I couldn't wait to find time to go to the hideaway again. Now that I knew the way and found my guide, I could enter the sacred silence with more ease. My guide was peaceful and strong but used very few words. Many times he would show me images that gave me helpful information instead of speaking. I learned there is nothing to fear in meditation, it cannot harm you because it is communication with Nature and the Divine.

Weeks later, I had a lot on my mind and needed to go to my sacred place to sort it out. I could not quiet my mind, so I returned to the drumming and looking at one spot until I calmed my mind enough to enter the silence. Eventually I realized that whatever works to quiet the mind is fine, that meditation and listening for guidance was everything. I used sacred silence to escape my family whenever I could. But as I grew older and my responsibilities grew, my meditations became less frequent. Over time the demands of everyday life became the priority and slowly I gave up the meditations.

After my NDE I remembered what I had learned and experienced in my foothills hideaway and realized it was only a beginning. Meditation is the cornerstone of many religions and beliefs, and through it we can achieve consciousness with Spirit and Nature. I recalled that the mind is not the enemy and I only needed to quiet it in order to open a channel of communication. Unlike what I had learned in youth, my mind, or what I call "Self," was now present in meditation, not set aside but at hand to focus on Spirit's message. Now I keep Self present when working with Spirit. In today's lifestyles, meditation needs to be more dynamic and usable. But I'll share more about that later on.

Testing, Testing

The supreme truths are neither the rigid conclusions of logical reasoning nor the affirmations of credal statement, but fruits of the soul's inner experience.

— *Sri Aurobindo*

Shortly after returning to life I started receiving information. At the time I called it a "download" or a "knowing" because I did not know what else to call it. As an engineer, I did not immediately trust these sudden knowings: Where did the information come from? It's not something I learned in training or in school. So,

I'd test the information I received. Questioning is a part of our humanness…and maybe a little of my obsessively self-controlled engineering side. A small amount of skepticism keeps things in a healthy balance.

Often these information downloads would come at the perfect time. For example, I would be aboard ship, working, and be confronted with an obstacle like a mechanical failure in one of the ship's systems. In an instant I'd understand the problem and see the solution, though it would be in a way that was totally foreign to my sphere of knowledge. Like one time a pump that supplied the ship's sprinkler system and fire hoses with saltwater stopped working. All indications pointed to a mechanical failure. Yet I was guided to open the intake and found a blowfish had been sucked up in through the screens and frightened he did what was natural and puffed up blocking the intake. He was glad to be out of there when I found him. Every time I acted upon this newfound knowledge, it proved accurate and assisted me in overcoming the obstacle faster than if I'd used my standard problem-solving techniques.

I distrusted these 'knowings' at the beginning because of the incredible scope of the subjects and issues they encompassed. The knowings ranged from repair solutions and job planning to having experiences with those around me. I would be having a quiet conversation with someone and suddenly I would intuit intimate information about that person. *"Oh my gosh, I can't share that!"* Then you find out *"Holy cow, it's all true!"* What do you do with that?

The only way I could keep my sanity and satisfy my engineering mind was to test these knowings. I know we all have little voices in our heads that tell us what constitutes our judgments. Yet that is not how a knowing would present itself. The knowing was a matter of fact, with no judgment or criticism attached to it. Over time, I became able to discern between a knowing and my mind chattering. Developing this ability to discern was a slow and sometimes emotionally painful process. My engineer's instinct to test proved beneficial. The judgments and criticisms my mind created were false, self-imposed illusions—self-defense against some imagined future failure. The knowings, on the other hand, were always accurate and to the point.

When people would ask how I'd become so insightful, I would brush it off with *"I had a hunch"* or *"Well, it comes with experience"*— when in fact it was the knowing that was the experience! I did my best to hide this new gift, and by now I was getting pretty good at concealing it. I still didn't feel I could share any of these esoteric gifts with others. My own fears kept me from opening up.

As I worked with my knowings and evaluated them, I came to rely on their truth. Knowings were not an all-the-time thing, either. They would come and go. I could not call upon a download on demand. So knowings remained helpful though an enigma.

Being of Service

All that we are is the result of what we have thought: it is founded on our thoughts, it is made up of our thoughts. If a man speaks or acts with an evil thought, pain follows him, as the wheel follows the foot of the ox that draws the carriage... If a man speaks or acts with a pure thought, happiness follows him, like a shadow that never leaves him.

— Gautama Buddha

At first I did not grasp that my physical and mental state would affect the connection to my new source of information. Much later I learned that when I am in a place of peace and centeredness knowings are more readily available, but in the beginning I was not very centered. In fact, I was swinging from one emotional extreme to another. But on the days that I was able to find my calm center, guidance was not far away. Indeed, I soon found that when things were at their worst, a clear sense of calm and focus would come over me. I became very good at crisis management as a result.

Even though I loved the sea, something was directing me away from my engineering work. I knew I had to go somewhere else. I didn't understand why, I just knew there was something else I had to do. Again I was confronted with a knowing only this one was more difficult to unravel.

The question of my purpose was haunting me as well. A driving need to be of service to my fellow man developed. As a consequence, the drive to leave the research vessel became so strong that it stirred my passions, and I became frustrated. I loved my job on the *Aloha*, but I spent so much time at sea that I felt too distant to be of assistance to mankind. Sometimes my emotions would surface as anger as a result of that frustration.

I have since learned that this need to be of service is common among experiencers. The International Association for Near-Death Studies (IANDS), which has been researching NDEs for over thirty years, publishes the peer-reviewed *Journal of Near-Death Studies*. A Fall 2006 journal article focused on NDE aftereffects, documented that 100 percent of experiencers in a study reported feeling changed by the experience and many felt a need to volunteer or work in a service organization. In the same study 65 percent of experiencers reported career changes.

My drive to be of service in combination with how my knowings were directing me left only one option, to leave my life on the research vessel. It wasn't long before a new job opportunity presented me with the ability to be of service to others.

Moving On

In the mountains of truth you will never climb in vain: either you will get up higher today or you will exercise your strength so as to be able to get up higher tomorrow.

— *Friedrich Nietzsche*

I left my life at sea for a job ashore. Opportunities for change started coming fast. First I began a new career as an engineer in the Ventura County Medical Center biomedical department. Then, a little more than a year later, my wife and I returned to Syracuse, New York, and I found work at St. Joseph's Hospital. From a chief engineer on a research vessel to a chief technician at a dialysis center was quite a jump and in a short period of time. Most of my friends could not understand how I made the transition. Again, I would make little of it, saying, *"The theory behind it is the same—they just use smaller tools!"* I was getting much better at concealing. I no longer had to work at hiding: my knowings had become automatic.

My three gifts and knowings helped me become a certified nephrology technologist in nine months. At the same time I was helping design a new water purification system and a hybrid bicarbonate delivery system. Guidance kept me in the right place at the right time, and although there was a lot of adversity in the new workplace, I advanced.

In this fast-paced logical environment I soon became one of the managers in the dialysis programs. Then Spirit showed me that the patients needed a more caring environment. The care that patients receive in clinical institutions is so sterile, white, and harsh. Also, focus was needed in the work environments. Smoother workflows for the clinicians contributed to a happier work atmosphere.

At first, I had no idea how I was going to accomplish this. I didn't even know what I was going to say when I went into planning meetings. I just started talking and the information came to me. I started to pitch my ideas about how patients would do better in treatment if the environment was more comforting. I was able to convince the directors and vice presidents that the environment of care for patients was just as important as the health care they received. I contributed to the planning of five new and remodeled dialysis centers, with an innovative focus on an environment for care. After the new centers were up and running, we got immediate positive outcomes. Patients responded well to the new environment which helped them to tolerate their treatments more effectively. We also found their hospitalization rates dropped significantly. I knew this is where I was supposed to be and I began to rely on my guidance.

My new line of work required so much more analytical thought that often I'd feel myself being pulled out of balance. I would swing away from my newly developing spiritual centeredness. I don't remember how exactly I got interested in cutting and polishing stones or wire-wrapping the stones into jewelry, but it helped me regain my center. I found I was able to bring that centeredness into my daily work life. With a newfound balance, more productivity at work followed. I was very much a workaholic and remain so to this day.

My jewelry-making hobby started out pretty small. I made some new friends who had the same interest and we joined the local lapidary club, the Gem and Mineral Society of Syracuse. I found that working with the stones was a way to find some quiet time where I could just focus on my creativity. Before I knew it, my hobby evolved into silversmithing. I never took any classes: I just knew how to do it. Again, I used the knowings to give me instructions. As a result, I had remarkably few failures, amazing, because I was sure some of the designs would never work. I started fabricating silver and making my own style of jewelry that incorporates stones and faceted gems in the design. Soon my hobby became a small side business.

Now my knowings began to present themselves as inspirations for new jewelry designs and concepts. Within quiet times in my shop, the knowings became clearer. Jewelry making became an exercise through which I could discern a clearer understanding of Spirit's instruction. When you work with your own creativity, you are closer to your heart and to your personal truth. Inspiration leads to being able to hear Spirit. Understanding what Spirit is trying to say becomes simpler when you are in touch with your creativity, unlike when we are involved with analytical thought.

When we use the analytical side of our brain, we are usually focused on details and the day-to-day needs of a situation. We are using our mind more than our heart. When you work with your creativity, you allow your mind and the day-to-day subjects to fall away, and you pay more attention to your heart's desires—your truth. When you are in that place, it is much easier to understand and connect with spiritual guidance. I believe that creativity is the doorway to inspiration, and that inspiration leads us to communicating with Oneness. I used these opportunities to fine-tune my guidance from what I now started calling "Spirit".

I had quite a bit of growth during this period of time at work and at play. At the same time, I started moving away from some friendships and toward others. I think this is natural when you are integrating a spiritual experience into your life. Some friends may leave your circle and others may step in. Some of your friends may exhibit behaviors and attitudes that you can no longer align yourself with. Instead of becoming confrontational and judging them, it is much easier to slowly distance yourself. Sometimes, on the other hand, you'll want to bring your friends along with you, but that's not always the way the world works. The world doesn't always beat to your drum. Since I was trying to become a more loving and accepting person, putting distance between myself and certain others was better than the alternative: pointing out our differences and trying to change them. That mode of "old me" behavior would only lead to confrontations, and worse, to bad feelings and an unhealthy separation.

You are never ever going to change some people. As much as you would like to, they don't have the capability or it may not be their time. You do try, you do not run away, but you get to a point when you realize that you cannot affect any change. You reach a point in the conflict where you just need to let it go and allow the person to follow his or her path, even if you don't agree with it. Bless them and wish them a good life path.

I had a friend who was dealing with an addiction. I tried to help him by setting him up in rehab and being supportive. He just could not get himself together. Kicking the drugs was beyond his ability at the time. To watch the situation was hurting me, especially when I was unable to correct it. I had to let it go, walk away, even though it broke my heart. It was a huge lesson for me. I watched as he lost everything, but I met him years later and he had rebuilt his life. It wasn't his time to change when I wanted to help. He needed to spiral down until he hit bottom before he could accept help.

At the same time I was trying unsuccessfully to help this friend, I found I no longer wanted to drink. That it clouded the knowing and my inspiration was unacceptable. I liked the clear communications I was receiving, which were not just helpful to myself but other folks were benefiting as well.

The near-death experience definitely changes you. Some of my friends saw how much I was changing and did not approve. Although it was troubling, I knew I had to allow them not to like it. Again I had to release my attachment and be tolerant of their paths. My NDE helped me see the world with a certain amount of detachment. This detachment was the root of more than a few misunderstandings. Detachment is not a lack of caring, rather, it helped me to comprehend what were other peoples issues. I learned to become a better observer.

Sometimes we involve ourselves in issues where we don't belong—we are off our path. Spirit taught me that we have to be tolerant of other people's paths because diversity is what makes up and strengthens a community. If we all had the same ideology, there would be no exchange of ideas, only stagnation.

A Call Home

We must know that we have been created for greater things, not just to be a number in the world, not just to go for diplomas and degrees, this work and that work. We have been created in order to love and be loved.

— *Mother Teresa*

Early one morning in February 1991 as I was waking and getting ready for work, I felt an overpowering call to return to the Light. I didn't understand what was happening. I had very little control with this summoning. I found myself just outside the Light, with my entire Soul Family. We were watching a Kuwaiti man as he was attempting to shut down an oil well fire after Allied Coalition Forces in Desert Storm had secured the area. The sky was choked by clouds of acrid black smoke from the hundreds of oil wells the Iraqis had torched as they retreated. The heat in the area of the fire was an inferno, so no one could get close to the well. Just then there was an eruption from the well head, sending scorching metal flying. My Soul Family and I watched as the Kuwaiti turned to run and a piece of metal struck him. It hit him at the base of the head where his red and-white headscarf was wrapped around his neck, knocking off his hardhat and killing him instantly.

His soul was out of his body before the metal ever hit him. He was looking down at his lifeless body. I now realized why I had been summoned: This man, Aadil, was part of my Soul Family and I had been called to welcome him as he returned home into the Light. His soul was disoriented from the sudden death. We were supporting Aadil by sending love, allowing him to reconnect to his true being. Once the totality of his Light being was with him he remained quizzical, inquiring about how this happened, mixed in with concern for his earthly family especially his eldest son. His earthly body was broken beyond repair and there was no returning to life for him.

We continued to send him pure love as he found the answers to his questions. Eventually he came to acceptance of the finality of his earthly life. My own physical emotions finally pulled me away from the Light and my Family. I missed my Soul Family and I felt this was cruel to subject me to Aadil's homecoming. I was conflicted by a powerful longing to return and living my life, trying to forget all of this.

As I experienced Aadil's death I realized I was the only one from my Soul Family who was still incarnated in this lifetime. Spirit confirmed this. I felt alone once more, so much so that I called in sick to work that day and the next. I needed that much time to emotionally calm myself. There was no one I felt comfortable with to talk to about this. My earthly family thought I was on the verge of a nervous breakdown. So again I used what was familiar and practiced, I pushed it down, got myself under control, not telling anyone about this call home.

I became involved in a non-denominational church in Upstate New York called Sanctuary of the Beloved with Revs. Daniel and Carol Chesbro. This spiritual group believed in the idea that multiple faiths and schools of belief can come together for spiritual growth. When I met this group, their acceptance resonated with the lessons of Acceptance, Tolerance and Truth. I started attending some of their spring retreats and summer conferences. In these gatherings I was able to explore other faiths and their spiritual connections and practices. Those retreats, with the fellowship and spiritual focus, refilled my cup and allow me to return to day-to-day living with renewed energy.

I did change quite a bit in the eleven years after my near-death. The gifts helped me immensely along the way. Although, my human ego had me believing that I was doing great, that was going to change. Its funny, how in life we seem to need some obstacles in our paths to overcome and many of the real life purposes are to conquer those obstacles.

Over time I began to be more understanding of different belief systems. Only when opportunities to study with medicine men and other natural healers suddenly appeared in my life's course did I turn in those directions. Serendipity certainly was playing its part in my life. If I was paying attention things went smooth, if I wasn't listening, or worse, ignoring what guidance was showing me then the dark clouds would crest on the horizon and the course would become much more difficult.

Chapter Five

❀ SOUL FAMILY RETURNS ❀

As a lump of salt thrown in water dissolves and cannot be taken out again, though wherever we taste the water it is salty, even so, beloved, the separate self dissolves in the sea of pure consciousness, infinite and immortal. Separateness arises from identifying the Self with the body, which is made up of the elements: when this physical identification dissolves, there can be no more separate self.
— *Brihadaranyaka Upanishad*

Eleven years after my near-death experience, just before Easter of 1994, my wife and I decided to attend a spiritual retreat in Sedona, Arizona, hosted by Sanctuary of the Beloved. I felt this was a great opportunity to return home to my old stomping grounds. I intended on spending time with the group, but my real plan was to hike the old trails of my youth. I love to hike, and I've always found it a great way to get in touch with my spiritual side. I couldn't wait to trek up to my meditation hideaway and other sacred spaces.

Excited at the prospect of returning to the actual locations, we packed our bags, flew to Arizona and met everyone at the Canyon Portal Motel. I really enjoyed this group of folks from all over the world and of many different religious beliefs, all with a common purpose—to grow spiritually. The first morning meditation was the next day at Bell Rock, and I planned to set aside the afternoon for a solo trek through some of the familiar canyons.

The next morning we convened at Bell Rock and were told to find a quiet place to center and meditate for a short period of time, then we would gather together. Great! I knew a nice secluded little place that felt like a secret grotto. So I skedaddled up to it and, feeling very comfortable, settled in like a bird in his nest. It was shaded by some mesquite and I had my back toward the red rock. To begin my meditation I planned to use techniques the grandmothers had taught me so long ago.

One technique they'd taught, to find my sacred space, was to visualize a path and follow it down into the earth. Along the way, to quiet the mind, I would imagine things like a cool stream and would listen to the water while continuing down that path, which opened up to a clear sky with beautiful clouds. I found myself floating above the landscape. This would take me to my sacred place. I usually find myself sitting on a plateau very much like the one from my youth looking out at the valley. The real physical location was the site I was looking forward to visiting again in the afternoon, but I always hold this sacred space within me. Once there in meditation I sit open eyed and just look across the valley. While doing this, my breathing would be rhythmic like a drum, synchronized with my heartbeat. This was usually when my guide would approach and stand behind or beside me. Most of the time he would show me a scene that played out in the valley or offer, without words, some wisdom that was needed. But this is not what happened that day at Bell Rock.

Return to the Light

As the builders say, the larger stones do not lie well without the lesser.
— *Plato*

In my grotto on Bell Rock, being at peace and comfortable with my surroundings, I went into deep meditation very quickly. As I was moving toward my sacred space, suddenly a very large, calm and loving voice, which seemed very familiar, told me, GO INTO THE LIGHT. I was shocked to hear Spirit talking. Not just a projected insight or guidance, Spirit was *talking*, the voice resonating with an incredibly deep love that I felt within me and surrounding me.

Although I had been meditating by means of finding my sacred space since I was fourteen, I had never heard a voice. Often you hear your own mind chatter, which you just allow to fade away, but I had never heard anything like this. It was more than just hearing. It was feeling, knowing and hearing. It was a voice that reverberated through my being. I recognized it at once as the same voice from the Light. The voice that told me it was time to return to life.

Before this, I had never thought it was possible to voluntarily return to the Light or make an effort to touch the Light in meditation. I always assumed that the place of "God's Light, the Universal All" was not a place for a mere mortal like me to meddle. Only ancient prophets and sages could enter the light of universal consciousness; no one nowadays speaks to that divine presence unless called there.

But now instead of going into my sacred space, I was hearing a voice and I found myself back in the ocean. I had already breathed in salt water and was in the process of dying and entering the dark void. My entire near-death scenario was being replayed. I had somehow kicked open the "do not touch" box that I had stuffed away in the back of my mind eleven years ago. I found myself back in the Light, back in the Love. I was back in the arms of total compassion. Although I had become a bit prideful in my three gifts over the years, I had forgotten the basis of how I received them. Now everything came flooding back again with the same powerful intensity. I relived the pain of death and the greater pain of returning to my body.

The most moving part was meeting my Soul Family again. I am the type of guy who is in control of emotion most of the time. But when I found myself in the Light my emotions rocketed out of control. The incredible longing to be with my soul group—my family, my home—racked my body with uncontrollable sobs. Overpowering waves of unconditional love and comfort made me as weak as a rag doll. My sobbing would not stop. I had no way to control it.

In my first near-death experience, I had perceived my Soul Family as welcoming me home, sending love and support as a single entity. I kept my focus on the original three light beings who greeted me. This time each member of my Soul Family emanated a more individual love and welcoming. They each had an individual flavor and essence. Light beings are stunningly beautiful, and powerful. The sight of them initially captivated me, blinding me to the full amount of detail in that experience.

Now, at Bell Rock I could not only see them clearer, I could also see myself better. I recognized that I too was a Light being, just like my Soul Family. I saw strength within my Light, a strength I do not carry within me in this life. I think that strength comes from the unbelievable amount of love and knowledge of my true being imparted by my Soul Family.

In the NDE itself and in this reliving of the near-death experience, I came to believe two aspects are what subsequently influenced my life the most; the life review along with my exposure to unconditional Love. These were the big bonks on the head I needed to change my life's direction and set a course to where I needed to be. The loving, nonjudgmental support during the reviews gave me the tools needed to change my life. This second time I was able to see more detail because I wasn't so much in wonder of the experience. That allowed me to comprehend so much more. The life review is an important area, so please excuse me if I spend more time on this subject.

In my life reviews I experienced an episode from my past I'm not proud of and I am hesitant to include here. Yet it illustrates the clarity I experienced in the second review. In 1975, living in Cottonwood, Arizona, I went to pick up my friend Mike, who was getting off work in Sedona. I was early, so I went to the Oak Creek Tavern to have a drink and kill some time. Back then it was an old cowboy bar, now it's called the Cowboy Club. I was sitting at the bar having a beer when a guy sat down next to me. Yet in the review, I was reliving the experience as me and I was watching the event from the bartender's view and the guy sitting next to me's perspective all at the same time. The Bartender was busy at the other end of the bar with his back to us, he was feeling tired. The guy next to me apparently had had a couple of drinks too many, because he leaned over to me and asked me to have sex with him. I instantly went into a vicious rage. All my life's frustrations churned up and furiously poured out of me, and I attacked him. At first he was feeling stunned, shock and confusion because he had misjudged the situation and me. He quickly tried to put up a defense as my fists came rapidly raining down pummeling him. I was caught up in my own cloud of anger and could not stop myself. The bartender called the sheriff, and was thinking, "It's too damn early to have a fight." Then the bartender came around and started pulling me off the man. Other men in the bar joined the bartender. I started screaming about how the guy had propositioned me. Everyone in the bar heard and I could feel the shifts in the emotions and the energies of the room.

When the fight started, beside what the three of us were feeling, the energy in the bar was quizzical, as people wondered what was going on. Then as I started yelling, the energy shifted, and negativity emanated from everyone in the bar toward this man. In the seventies Sedona was still a western town with many of the accompanying prejudices and discriminations. As I was dragged kicking and screaming outside, I could feel everyone connected through common hatred, similar to a mob mentality. The bruised man lowered his face and was feeling shame from the weight of the negative energy and focused his hatred back toward me.

When the sheriff arrived he spoke to the bartender first then approached me. I could see in his eyes that he was planning to admonish me. Before he could speak, I spit out my version of what happened, and he too got caught up in the discrimination. Instead of charging me as he'd planned, he said he would only do it if the victim pressed charges. The man I'd beat up was so shaken by the event that all he wanted to do was get away from the bar and everyone, more concerned with how the knowledge of him being gay would go over in the community. Eventually, another patron who mumbled agreement for my actions gave me my hat and then I left.

I relived this experience, watching the event from the bartender's as well as the victim's perspective, all at the same time. The intensity of the energy and the connection to so many people amazed me. I clearly experienced the entire interactions of everyone, what they were feeling and what their life energy went through. I felt shame as my Soul Family experienced this episode of my life review with me. As I've stated before, my Soul Family had no judgment. We experienced the embarrassment the man went through as the community came to know of his homosexuality. Eventually he used the experience to go public with his lifestyle. In the end the reverberations from the Sedona experience led him to another community where he was accepted.

I'm still not happy with the way I acted that day. I know I would never move toward violence today; in fact, I detest the use of violence. I no longer fear alternative life styles and many of my friends are members of the gay community. This one event in my life strengthened my resolve to allow others to live their lives and travel their life's paths and follow their purpose. I saw how our purposes can be interconnected for just the briefest of moments and yet have the most significant impacts. We come and go from so many people's lives. Often we never get to know or see any outcomes. (Fortunately, Sedona has also grown since the seventies and now is a much more rich and diverse community that I enjoy returning to each year.)

Due to the increased clarity in this second life review, I was able to see more of the ripples and effects of my actions. I re-experienced my side of the interaction, and I experienced how my actions affected the other person. If I was hurtful to that person, I felt the hurt they experienced and saw how they carried it with them. I also saw how my loving intentions played forward.

Eleven years ago, in my first life review, I had been confused when I was shown events in my life that had not yet taken place. But now, on Bell Rock, I could breathe life into many of those events. From this new vantage point, I was able to see the changes I had effected within myself by utilizing my gifts of Acceptance, Tolerance and Truth over years. I saw how I had grown and changed after the first experience. In those years, I had consciously attempted to make myself a better person. I watched the results of living in a more consciously loving manner.

Don't get me wrong, I still have a lot of room for improvement. I certainly am not hanging a halo on my bedposts at night. But during this experience, I was not judged by my family of Light and felt total, unconditional Love and Acceptance.

Slivers of Light

> But the truth is, the sun's beams strike the wall, and the wall only reflects that borrowed light… GO! Seek the source of light which shineth always!
>
> — *Rumi*

There is more I want to say about what I encountered in the second life review. In reliving my actions I saw how I touched others through an energetic interconnection. We all give off energy that reflects our emotional and mental state. This interconnectedness is actually a form of conscious communication perceived by our souls.

I saw this energy as slivers of light that connect us to one another and to our True Beings. I've heard it referred to by others as divine cords. I saw the exchange on three different levels: energetic, cellular and molecular. We constantly have these additional forms of communication interacting with all life around us. This communication is happening all the time even when we are asleep.

I observed the more erratic the state of our mind and emotions, the more inconsistent the message being delivered will be. Also, the level of our passion directly correlates with the intensity of the energy exchange of our message. It doesn't matter whether the passion is love or hate. The slivers of light are brighter and stronger when our passion level rises. I realized that if we can learn to discipline our mind, these interconnected communications would be less inconsistent and more focused. The larger lesson here is that, this interconnectedness exists between all living beings and the Divine Consciousness at all times. We are always connected to everyone else. We do not have to be in the physical presence of someone to have an energetic exchange that affects his or her life.

Just like in the first life review, I gained a greater knowledge and understanding of anything I focused on. It was necessary to relive my NDE a second time to remind me of all that I'd tried to push away in the experience eleven years ago. The most important revelation was the acceptance of God's Light in my being. The first time I couldn't face it—accepting God's Light was simply too much for me, overwhelming me. I did not feel worthy of the experience. But, after these years of working with my gifts of Acceptance, Tolerance and Truth, I gained the tools I needed to finally accept the experience of God's Love and Light. I was now able to see that my True Being is a part of the Light connected to the greater All of God. My True Being has access to all the love and knowing of the Universal Mind. All of us are able to connect to our True Beings through Spirit to help us achieve our Purpose, Purpose, Purpose.

My Spirit sang with gladness to be in the loving joy of the Light, but at the same time my human side knew I was on this earth. I relived my near-death experience entirely, but instead of coming back into my body in the swirling ferocity of a Pacific storm, I found myself sitting on Bell Rock. At least I didn't have to make that swim back to shore again!

God Sent Me Richard

None but the sun can display the sun, If you would see it displayed, turn not away from it. Shadows, indeed, may indicate the sun's presence, But only the sun displays the light of life… Naught but Love itself can explain love.

— Rumi

Coming out of my meditation, I was shaking, soaked in sweat and tears—as if I really had been in the ocean. I tried to get myself together and return to the group, but instead I wandered to and fro a bit to try to compose myself (gotta be in control, y'know). The experience and the Light were still with me and my heart was painfully wide open as I slowly gathered my strength. I stumbled on wobbly legs down Bell Rock, on my way back to the group's gathering place.

But then, a few yards away from the group I ran across Richard. He was smiling, though when he saw me became concerned. I think he instantly saw the stress I was under and probably felt my energetic call for help. I had to try to say something, to communicate about this encounter. I tried to explain what I had just gone through. I was nervous, fearing rejection and criticism once more. I was having trouble finding the right words. Richard was a good friend with Tom Sawyer, a well-known near-death experiencer from Rochester, New York (and yes, that was his real name). Richard had heard Tom's accounts firsthand and had many discussions with Tom about the experience. This gave Richard a vocabulary, and he calmly put a name to my experience. He told me I'd had a near-death experience.

"There is a name for this? There are others that have gone through this?" Remember, though I use the term in this book in recounting my experiences, up until that day in 1994, I thought I was alone.

Richard's acceptance was a vast relief. It gave my mind some peace to know that my experience wasn't such a strange thing. He helped me to calm myself and that in return helped my heart to stay open. Although we were only a short distance from the group, everyone left us alone. They could probably tell some kind of counseling was going on. Besides, they were all caught up in their own discussions.

My newly named experience would not leave me alone; it was consistently at the forefront of my thought process and my being. For three days I kept reliving it. Sometimes it would just be the death. Another time it was the Light or the Soul Family and next time maybe a part of my life review. Every time I would glean a little more understanding. I kept getting pushed back into that place where I was half here in physical presence with my heart wide open and half there in my light body.

Whenever my thought would linger on an aspect of my NDE, I would relive that part of my experience again. My emotions were so elevated and raw from the constant exposure of Love that I could experience a full range of intense emotions at any moment. I tried not to think about the NDE so much, to force my mind to think about the beauty of Sedona's magnificent red rocks, the feel of the sun on my face, or the warm breeze blowing across the mesquite trees, but the knowledge of the interconnection with the Divine would take me back into the Light again.

The most wonderful thing, and at the time the most disconcerting, was that I could now hear Spirit as a warm, resonating voice within my being. Spirit was now talking to me as I kept reliving my near-death experience. To say I was having trouble getting used to this new form of communication was an understatement. I was totally freaked out.

Needless to say during these three days I didn't get to go hiking. All my wonderful plans had to be put on hold. It was terrible… no, it wasn't terrible, it was *wonderful*. But it was also frightening and emotionally draining. I got very little sleep during those three days because I couldn't shut it off. I was worried that I'd finally went over the edge and that they were going to put me away in an institution. I thought, "This is really NOT GOOD, I cannot live this way."

I spent a good deal of time alone. I needed to be away from the others. My wife, though concerned, was unable to deal with or be around me while I was in and out the NDEs. She didn't know what to do so she stayed with the group. The leaders of the group, Dan and Carol Chesbro understood and recommended she give me the space I needed. We were so close, but here I was changing before her eyes. The extra space meant I did not have to participate in every activity the group was doing. There were no hard and fast rules with this group and for that I was thankful.

Richard was able to listen to me without any baggage, since he barely knew me; he just allowed me to get it out and let it happen. Richard helped me put some words to my experience. Checking in on me a couple times during the trip, he was an immense help. He didn't even know how much help he was that day. I guess he'll see it in his life review right? Then he'll know all the ripples that he caused.

Many years later, in January 2005, I was asked to share my experiences with the IANDS group in Rochester by Chuck Swedrock, who founded the group. When I reached the point in my story about Richard, I was surprised to spot him sitting in the back of the room. Afterward Richard and I talked about that day, and I was even more surprised to hear him confess that as much as he wanted to help me, and even as he did, he also was experiencing an urge to play

a nearby-unattended guitar. He felt guilty that he hadn't given me his full attention and until now had no idea how much of a cornerstone his acceptance had
become in my integration. He was blown away to hear the significance of that
little bit of aid he rendered. Now he won't have to wait until his own life review
to know that a little assistance to another can create an enormous amount of
positive energy.

It was empowering to have such a receptive audience in Richard since I did not
receive that after the first NDE. Gaining a vocabulary from Richard helped my
mind start to process the experience and evaluate it. As I popped in and out of the
Light over those three days in Sedona, I kept trying to gain a better understanding and feeling of the experience. The small, positive seed that Richard planted
helped me through those next weeks and months and continued to grow over the
years. It allows me to communicate more openly about the experience and not
keep it all locked up inside.

Let the Integration Begin

*When a man dies, what does not leave him? The voice of a dead
man goes into fire, his breath into wind, his eyes into the sun, his
mind into the moon, his hearing into the quarters of heaven, his
body into the earth cheerfully, his spirit into space.*
— *Brihad-Aranyaka Upanishads*

By the end of the third day in Sedona I started to get it. Sometimes Spirit has to
hit me over the head very hard. The initial three gifts I had been working with
kicked in and I began to accept the entire near-death experience. I needed a buf-
fer period before I could accept that I had been in God's hands. If I just listened,
Spirit would speak to me. I also learned you can live your life with an open heart
and listen through your heart instead of your mind.

Having your heart wide open is not only a physical experience, in which you
can actually feel an ache in your chest area, it is also an emotional experience.
After you return from the Light, your heart expands and you are aware of celes-
tial communication, which resonates on a soul level, stimulating our emotions.
Information doesn't filter through the mind, it comes in big clumps through your
heart. It is up to our emotions to deal with the full impact of that information.

This communication is the unconditional love that you receive while in the
light and you can feel the Love reaching out for everything around you. Your
mind cannot immediately conceptualize this type of communication into a single limited physical idea. Also when that reality comes through the heart and is

experienced directly, it overwhelms the physical emotions. I believe this is why experiencers need to integrate their experience a little at a time. Otherwise all the emotion and interconnectedness becomes overwhelming. Overcoming our emotional limitations and building our ability to cope is a long process. I wish I could say I was ready at that time to face the light again. I see now that my own fears had blocked me from learning all of this the first time.

Another gift I received from the Light—and which pushed me to the edge of questioning my sanity!—was being able to look into others' eyes and see their Light. It is the Spirit Light that connects them to their True Being. This is an incredibly intimate exchange between souls, so much so I was embarrassed to see someone's Spirit light without permission. It felt so intrusive. You can imagine how conflicted I was. On one hand I didn't want to invade someone's privacy, and on the other, everyone's Light is so magnificent to experience. It got so bad I was afraid to look people in the eyes unless we were communicating about spiritual concerns. Fortunately, the group in Arizona was an assembly of spiritually focused individuals, thus giving me a week's worth of cushion in trying to get a handle on it all.

Over time I adjusted, and can now look at someone and not see his or her Light unless I direct my focus toward it. I find it is much easier to see another experiencer's Spirit Light, which makes it easier to recognize each other.

Eventually I was able to rejoin the group and take some wonderful hikes. A small group of us broke away one afternoon making our way to one of my sacred meditation spots. One of the hikers, Lou Budell, and I shared afterward and discovered that our meditations were interwoven with each other's. It left us with the feeling that we had been brothers in some past life together. We both sensed an exchange of energy and interconnectedness between us. That was a reminder that the unconscious energetic communication and interconnectedness I experienced in my NDE is happening in life all the time.

During another meditation that day, I saw one of the guides of my youth. This was the first time I "saw" him face-to-face. I've always perceived him behind or beside me. When I felt his powerful spirit, I assumed he was a big and powerful being. But when I saw him face to face, he was a short, old gray-haired Indian. Although small, he still emanated a raw, steel-like resolve and presence, solid and immovable. His essence is so much bigger than his being presented to me. To me he is "Grandfather Mountain," small in size but not in presence.

Not long before our Sedona trip, I met with a Native American seer, Ted Silverhand, who told me that I was going to meet my guide on a deeper, more personal level. Grandfather Mountain, standing face to face with me, was a confirmation. The seer also spoke to me of one of my most important life paths: communication. Now that I could hear Spirit, directly, Spirit confirmed this message as well.

Communication doesn't always mean that I have to be talking to a large audience communicating a lesson of Light. When I am in my spiritual truth and centered, interconnection allows a deeper bond to form than just talking. I could communicate just as well one on one and touch people more profoundly. I saw this happen with the small group I took to my sacred place. We turned a hike into an intensely bonding spiritual journey. I enjoyed sharing this sacred space from my teenage years, and the seed for my quiet ministry was planted on that day. The incredible spiritual growth I found in Sedona had left me with a compulsion to change my life once again. I needed to achieve wholeness between my physical self and my attachment to my Light and the connection to the All One—God.

Spirit had indicated, "Time for change is coming"— and indeed I was ready.

Chapter Six

❀ QUIET MINISTRY ❀

We do not need to proselytize either by our speech or by our writing. We can only do so really with our lives. Let our lives be open books for all to study.

— *Mohandas Gandhi*

After returning back east from Sedona, I knew that I could do more to make myself a better person. I was determined to walk in a more respectful manner to the earth and live my life more compassionately. I now realize that a goal for living is more than just trying to understand spirituality and our connection. We need to live it every moment. Spirit was guiding me to understand this new concept, as well as helping me effect enough change within that I started living the concept.

My new way of life caused a large shift; I was changing one week to the next. My truth and philosophy were changing as I was growing. I no longer maintained two separate paths of my work life and my spiritual life because I could see where the two paths joined together. Although granted, I still had a lot of stones in my path and obstacles to overcome.

As I moved forward and got closer to the center of my path, I could hear Spirit more clearly. At first it wasn't all the time. The voice would come when I was trying to make a decision that was critical to my path. I would then receive some sort of guidance from Spirit that would help me make the right decision. Hearing Spirit actually talking was different than the 'downloads' or 'knowings' I had become accustomed to in the past. Although I still received those, the obstacle I faced now was trusting in Spirit and my new level of communication.

Obstacles are dealt with in many ways. You can step over them, but more than likely they will get under your feet, like stones on a road. You can sidestep them, but they really are not going away. Obstacles will always be in your path, and one method of dealing with them is pretending they do not exist, not looking at them. Yet Spirit will let you keep hitting them or stumbling over them until you open your eyes. You could even try to run away, or take a different path in order to sidestep the problem. In my life, the Universe just made sure that the obstacle rolled over me, making me deal with it.

Acknowledging the obstacle is the first step. You can then begin to see it in your path clearly and understand it. The best action is to look at it closely and not close your eyes. Try to learn as much as you can about your obstacle. Why is it in your path? What strength can you gain from overcoming it? Does this obstacle push some of your buttons? If so, explore why. When you truly understand everything about your obstacle, you can overcome it. These experiences are what will help you to evolve and grow. A good number of times we outgrow our life's obstacles.

I spent a great amount of time working on my quiet ministry. What I mean by "quiet ministry" is trying to live my life so that it serves as an example. I knew my life was going to cause ripples—I saw that in my life review. So, I decided to live my life with the knowing and acceptance of Spirit's communication and guidance. I found that having Spirit communicating with me was one of the most profound aspects of developing my quiet ministry. I spent time getting to understand this communication and passing the wisdom along.

I wasn't ready to share with others how I could hear Spirit yet; I just worked quietly. The more I worked on my ministry, the more I was able to hold my heart open. It's funny how people can sense your open heart and respond to it. They may not understand what it is, but they can feel it. So they begin to seek you out.

I met some wonderful teachers along the way at conferences and through other searching, people who helped me with my own spiritual integration and where my path lay. My circle began to include those with stronger belief systems. One teacher I sought out was Tom Sawyer, whom I met at a retreat after Sedona. He was giving a talk about his NDE. As he was speaking about his time in the Light I started to sob and sob. I couldn't help myself. I went into the bathroom to splash cold water on my face, which helped some. I returned to the lecture, and the sobs resumed. I saw Richard watching and he gave me a nod of recognition. Other attendees tried to comfort me but that didn't help either.

After the talk, I purchased Tom's book *What Tom Sawyer Learned From Dying,* because I wanted to know more about others who had an NDE. But I found I couldn't read it. Emotion would overwhelm me and I would have to put it down. I decided I would not read any books on NDEs. I had to work on this in my own way until I was ready.

At another conference, I was reintroduced to the tradition of pipe ceremony. I took it upon myself to undergo a spiritual journey in making my own pipe. I purchased some pipestone working with it by hand until it showed me how to form my pipe. As I worked the red stone many insights were revealed to me. The circle or hoop is a sacred symbol representing many things in life. Like your individual life, your family, community, and the whole earth. When performing the pipe ceremony it caused me to look at my cycles. We all have cycles in our life, and I think it's very important that we try to understand them. Some people's cycles are based on their birth, so every year on their birthday they begin a new cycle and end an old one. My cycles are not based on my birthday, nor are they based on my near-death date. My cycles begin in and around Thanksgiving each year. I noticed that my mother had a similar time of transition.

Working with the pipe, I began to feel cyclic changes in my energy. I became more sensitive to the energy shifts in my life. At the beginning of every cycle, I experienced a shift. Often shifts can be chaotic, because you're leaving a familiar energy and moving into a new unknown energy. Native Americans talk about cycles having a progression. Because each cycle may have a different energy it takes time to tune in to the new vibrations. Occasionally, you may repeat a cycle. You may not recognize it at first, but over time you will come to know it as an energy you have experienced before.

Silversmith

You will know that the divine is so great and of such a nature that it sees and hears everything at once, is present everywhere, and is concerned with everything.

— Socrates

I mentioned in chapter Five that I never had to study silversmithing, I just allowed Spirit to show me how. With a need to work with my hands to create something, I discovered my passion for jewelry making and silversmithing, using gemstones and natural elements to create something beautiful to share with others. Now that I could actually hear Spirit, I explored casting. I continued to see how making jewelry helped me to better define my communications with Spirit. Spirit showed me techniques and influenced my styles. I began to sculpt designs in wax and then cast them. I had never tried to sculpt anything before, so when Spirit wanted to go down this path I had some trepidation.

Sometimes Spirit would be so insistent about creating something that I couldn't create anything else until I followed the guidance. For example, I wasn't very interested in mixing different media like copper and brass with silver, nor had I developed any techniques for it. But Spirit kept showing me visions of small sculptures to create made from copper, bronze and brass sheets. I didn't want to do it; I was into silver. But then I found I wouldn't find inspiration for my silversmithing until I sat down at my bench and created these sculptures. The first one I made won a first-place ribbon at a local art contest. I put a fairly high price on these sculptures, figuring no one would want them. Besides, I thought I was making them for my own development and spiritual journey. But when I put them out for sale, they were snatched up right away. Customers would say, *"This is something I just have to own."* It was as if Spirit knew people needed those sculptures. It showed me there is more to the big universal picture that is beyond my perception. As soon as I completed the series, inspiration for my silver jewelry returned. This was only one of many confirmations I received that it was okay to trust in Spirit and the new way we communicated

Working with Spirit and with my creativity led me to meet others on similar spiritual paths. Looking back at this part of my life I see a series of synchronicities. I would never have gotten to know, interact and exchange with these people and eventually form lasting friendships with many of them if not for jewelry making. I count myself blessed to have met them.

Mindfulness

For, as the physical body is but a temple, each portion must coordinate one with another for a perfect union or perfect unison of service or activity, so must the mental mind, the physical mind, the spiritual mind, coordinate as one with another.

— *Edgar Cayce*

As I tried to integrate my new form of communication and insight into my life I discovered Buddhism's "mindfulness." Mindfulness is a part of the interconnection we have to everyone and everything in our universe. It's being able to touch that interconnection, yet not in the same way we touch something with our hand.

Buddhist thought paralleled many of my Native American beliefs and fit my quiet ministry well. You can develop mindfulness in a number of places doing any number of things. Walking, sitting, standing, working or resting are all practice opportunities. You need to be mindful to find the calm center within you. I like to tell myself that being mindful helps me to be here where "I am," in this present moment, because in the next moment it will only be a dream of the past. So being mindful is being aware of yourself and everything around you, at any given moment.

I had to start slowly to become mindful. I needed to be patient and gentle with myself, for it is a life's work. Mindful living is not something to master after going to one class. On a retreat for work I was reminded that we are only human and we are fallible. That allowed me to work on mindfulness, slowly allowing the practice to become a way of life.

Being present in this moment, the moment we are in, is when we are truly awake. We have everything we need. We no longer need to fear *"am I being the best person I can be?"* Fear only increases the mind chatter anyway. Spirit once told me, *"We are one flicker away from being awake. The flame on the candle is only there for the moment it has air, fuel, and heat. The flame must live in the moment."*

Developing mindfulness is multi-stepped. Finding your center, your sacred space, or stillness is one of the first steps you have to learn. I used my center for a number of years and thought that was all there was. I didn't realize there was more to the practice, although finding the quiet within you, in meditation, is reasonably fulfilling.

It is a natural progression to go from meditation to practicing mindfulness. I used Nature at first as an observation technique all the while maintaining my center, my stillness. I found ways to be alone with nature to observe her actions. Nature surrounds us with animals, insects, birds, wind in the leaves and water flowing over rocks. You don't need to be in wilderness; you can observe things like the sun coming up or the wind whirling in a suburban park. In the Northeast you can watch a squirrel out your back window. Observe how squirrels are so industrious, how they create their own environment and prepare for life's needs on an instinctual level. Notice their behavior as they interact with Nature.

Observation will develop your skills of awareness. You begin to hone your awareness by watching and observing how the natures of things work together. Then you expand your comprehension, relating events happening in your life to your new awareness or understanding. You'll begin to truly experience day-to-day happenings more fully.

I found that in order to expand my awareness, I first had to learn how to observe without judging or analyzing. Simply observe how things work and relate to each other. Try not to analyze. When analysis starts, it engages your mind and your mind will fabricate all types of misleading falsehoods. What you want to do instead is open your mind to understanding what really *is*. What are you really seeing? The mind tends to judge and turn pure observation into something else. We try to create our experience to fit something we need or to avoid opening up to something new. How do things work together without using your mind to add or take away?

Accept don't expect. Observation goes hand in hand with learning another life lesson, acceptance, because you have to accept what you purely observe. Some things in Nature are unpleasant, like a hawk catching a pigeon and eating it. This may seem unpleasant to some people, but it is a natural way of life. We tend to judge things as good or bad in varying degrees, depending on how much we like or dislike the situation. Try not to attach judgment, simply observe and understand what you are seeing, as it is. The hawk needs to eat and he catches the weak and slowest, making the flock stronger. Not judging is the first step in training your mind to be more positive.

When you observe nature you come back with a peaceful heart because, for just a little while, you have let go of judgments. We can't all be wearing brown robes and sandals, but we can stop clinging to our opinions like we cling to our possessions. Try to see things a little clearer and without so much judgment. We find more peace and love when we let go of our critical side.

You can also be mindful while observing other people. Take a bench seat in the park or mall and people-watch. Try watching children at the playground without judgment. Don't judge that one child is a bully or one is faint of heart. Just watch kids and observe their nature. It's more complicated to watch fellow humans rather than nature because of the energetic interactions. A crowd of people can generate a mob mentality because of our interconnectedness. Group energies can vibrate with each other and create a mass vibration that can knock you off your center and pull you in. Make sure, in crowds, to observe without judgment because if you pick up on mass energy you'll have trouble staying centered. When observing people, you might want to start with a less crowded environment, like a nature center or sacred site where people are more grounded.

As I develop more mindfulness, I've found that I have to let go of expectations. Even at a dinner party with friends, I have expectations they'll act certain ways and do certain things, especially as we become more familiar. Many times our expectations are our own projection. Do we really know friends and coworkers so well that we can predict every action?

We trip over ourselves by worrying about how someone else is doing his job or living her life. We are just hurting ourselves. They will always be either above or below our expectations. People are never going to do things the way you expect. Their truth is different than your truth. You need clear communication to come up with a result that is satisfactory to all of you. Expectation is just another type of judgment. With observation, you begin to see a person's true self, not a projection of your expectations. This allows healthier interaction.

I don't recommend observing other people as your primary way to develop mindfulness because there are too many variables. Yet, once you have worked with mindfulness enough that you can remain in your center, observing others is a good way to release expectations.

I had to work a while with observation in my mindfulness practices before I was ready to expand my awareness. Being a professional diver, I had experience with focusing on my breathing. In diving your breath control is an indicator of how you are doing in your work. Breathing hard means you are working too hard and using up your resources. We always keep a little focus on our breath. So, it was easy and natural for me to use breath in awareness practices. I started by using that same breath focus in daily activities. When doing this, I developed a sense of calm and centeredness that brought me to an awakened meditative state even during activity. I would concentrate my focus, centering attention on my breath and the activity. At the same time, using my new observation skills, applying non-judgment and understanding to my chosen activity.

While practicing this new level of mindfulness I began to have a greater awareness of everything around me. I started to comprehend the entire scope of whatever I was doing. I was expanding my focus through observation, the ability to understand without judgment, and maintaining my center. Bringing these skills one by one into an activity, I was able to focus on more than one thing at a time. Some recent studies say that we are not really multitasking; our brains just shift faster between activities. I agree with the studies, I found that I couldn't multitask with my brain alone. I need to be focused, centered and using my whole being, thus awakening other senses that tap into our interconnection.

Let's go back to being in the woods. If you are walking through the woods first focus on your breath, breathing in and breathing out, inhaling and exhaling. Once you have a steady, calm focus on your breathing, extend your focus to the rhythm of your steps. As you do this, you will notice that your breathing will slow and there will be more steps to each breath. Your stamina will be increased as you go farther with less effort. You can add a mantra to further develop that focus: *"As I breathe in, I breathe in Beauty" "As I breathe out, I breathe out my Truth."*

The words, the steps, and breaths all synchronize in your focus. For that moment in time, you are present. As you continue walking in the woods you will notice how you are now flowing with nature all around you. You are no longer just stomping your way through…you are a part of the natural flow. You can practice this in all sorts of activities. When you expand your focus on your breath, action, movement, and mental activity, it brings all these elements together to do whatever activity you have chosen in a mindful way.

Mindfulness is easier to achieve with simple tasks at first, like walking, gardening, or cleaning. The more you concentrate on this level of mindfulness, there will come in due course an expansion of your awareness. Your focus will grow outside of yourself. It's hard to explain, but you will become aware of more than just what you are focusing on. Your awareness will start to include your total surroundings. Eventually, you'll even become aware of cause and effects, the deeper understanding that is the true goal of mindfulness.

You must avoid judging your progress, because this level of ability doesn't happen overnight. Mindfulness starts as a discipline before it grows into being a way of life. We are all seekers and we all need practice, just as a great pianist still needs to rehearse.

Living the Mission

The purpose of life is not to be happy. It is to be useful, to be honorable, to be compassionate, to have it make some difference that you have lived and lived well.

— *Ralph Waldo Emerson*

How could I find my purpose if I wasn't true to myself at all times? I was training my mind to be open to endless possibilities, so why not insert it into all of my life? As a result, part of my quiet ministry was to bring my new discipline of mindfulness into my work, play and every other aspect of my life.

I tried to remain open to new ideas, even looking at old ideas and past events in life I thought I completely understood from a fresh perspective. I tried not to automatically say, *"I know."* Instead I would wonder, what more is there to know by opening a mental gap? Knowledge is necessary to think as well as evaluate, making it helpful in our daily lives. But there is a higher truth that is blocked by knowledge. Truth is found in living life, open to all possibilities. Our minds can chatter to such a point that we cannot hear our higher truth.

Within the hospital where I worked we had "Thoughts for the Month." One, was a quote from Buddhism which was cited by Mahatma Gandhi. His grandson Arun Gandhi said he was made to memorize and consciously implement this wisdom in his life, and it so struck me I turned it into a mantra for my practice.

Keep your thoughts positive because your thoughts become your words.
Keep your words positive because your words become your behaviors.
Keep your behaviors positive because your behaviors become your habits.
Keep your habits positive because your habits become your values.
Keep your values positive because your values become your destiny.

I started with only one line, and repeated it as often as I could for the first few days. After a few days, I found that saying the mantra became easier and more meaningful. Over time I found that my thoughts became more positive. I then moved on to the next line, and so on. I have been working on this mantra for over fifteen years and I am still working on the second and third line. Spirit recently asked me to amend the second line to "*I will speak impeccably so my words are not misunderstood.*"

Through the years of observing others, and myself, I found we often forget what we do or say, but long afterwards the results do catch up to us. By then we are unable to connect the results with their causes, positive or negative. I know I may not see the results of my actions now, but I will eventually.

A mantra can be used for many reasons. I use a mantra to open that mental gap, that sense of wonder. Then the gap becomes larger than life and unexplainable. It becomes the key to the Oneness, the Universal Consciousness. That sounds awful lofty, but when it happens, you know it is Truth.

The mantra I use the most is, "Great Spirit, thank you for this life." Sometimes I say it in native tongue, *"Wakan Tanka, pilamiya wilchoni hey"* I use it daily as I wake to start my prayers, my gratitudes, and when anything touches my heart. The Buddhist tradition calls that gap emptiness but I find it is emptiness with the warm energy of *"love is everything and everything is love."* The warmth of compassion dwells in that space and treats every encounter with gentleness.

Mindfulness develops seeing the interconnection between us and everything else in the universe. When you start to expand your awareness, you are reaching out and saying, *"I am ready and preparing myself for a connection to the universe."* *"I have cleaned my terminals."* You're getting ready to plug in. I became aware that everything in the universe does not evolve around me and that there is a lot more going on. We all have a place and purpose in the Oneness.

I began to see and experience more of the interconnection, how everything relates to everything else. Mindfulness is more than just being mindful of our thoughts. Being mindful is developing self into a more peaceful, calm human who walks in a peaceful manner with respect and gratitude. Mindfulness is a way of living, not just of thinking. It is being aware of self as well as others around you. Mindfulness is a way to develop self into a better being.

As my awareness expanded, I was able to see the natural flow of others, which allowed me to be aware of people's needs. For example, if you are in a service industry, you can observe the other person as well as his or her environment and provide what is really needed. Taking time to be more mindful helps you to eliminate steps and actions, and slowing down increases your awareness of others so you can be more supportive. When I am mindful of another's energies I can participate in that person's experience without becoming caught up in it.

Another thing mindfulness does is strip away the false persona we cloak self in. We spend a lot of time creating a *persona* so someone will either like us or leave us alone. Fear is one of the motivators to create this cloak, or persona. In mindfulness, you are trying to find your true self. You are trying to work from your own center. In order to accomplish that, you have to let go of false personas, allowing your true self to shine through.

I found that people became more comfortable around me because I was not confusing or unreachable. My interactions with others became more genuine. The more I was able to observe, the better I became at allowing people to be where they were on their path, even though I might not agree with them. I found that even in a conflict, I was able to distance myself and use *discernment* instead of judgment to help me decide if I wanted to interact or not.

The lack of judgment in my life reviews brought me to explore the difference between judgment and discernment. I found that in discernment, you are not adding labels. You are not seeing it as good or bad, you are saying, *"Is this a part of my path? Or is this something I do not need to be involved in."* Through discipline it simply becomes perception in the absence of judgment.

As I moved along on my quiet ministry I was often reminded to go back to the basics and review. As I started working on the higher levels, I found it easy to forget the simple rule of keeping yourself centered.

Your Stuff, Their Stuff

> *He who fights with monsters should look to it that he himself does not become a monster. And when you gaze long into an abyss the abyss also gazes into you.*
>
> — *Friedrich Nietzsche*

Mindfulness helped me to see when others were trying to add their obstacles to my path. I realized that I didn't have to own everyone else's "stuff," in the sense of their burdens. Man, was that a load off my shoulders! Although I must emphasize that I was not and am not always able to maintain this level of mindfulness for long periods. Yet, the benefits of mindfulness keep me striving to perfect this practice so I may maintain it longer.

I had a friend who was in a relationship with a person addicted to drugs and alcohol. Because she was so close to the situation, she was unable to separate his addictions from herself. She took his addiction on as her burden: he would blame her and she would believe it, accepting his projections. It wasn't until after she was able to see his addictions as separate, and not belonging to her, that she was able to let go of guilt he projected on her. Then they were able to deal with his issues successfully.

We tend to get wrapped up in other people's accusations, and so often it involves their expectations of us, or projecting on us. Developing mindfulness has allowed me to see this more clearly, and now I avoid taking on others' issues. Some might view you as distant or detached when you do this, but it's actually you seeing clearly and not connecting to the drama. Have you ever had a major situation in your life where you felt defeated and hurt, and then without knowing why you just let go of it? The frustration just goes away, and you wonder why you made so much of it. Well, the more you practice mindfulness, the more you can lighten up, or light up, with gentle solutions. Just sitting and being gentle with self allows rediscovering something more about you.

I spent quite a while getting to the point where I understood all this and began to pass it along in my quiet ministry. I saw how people were affected by the way I approached working with them and then watched how they used the tools of mindfulness in their lives. I didn't have to preach a sermon. Our interconnectedness was the vehicle of communication. Many of my coworkers and friends adopted a mindful approach and their lives turned in a more positive direction.

The more I worked on my quiet ministry, the more I was able to hold my heart open. It's funny how people can sense your open heart and respond to it. They may not understand what it is, but they can feel it. So they begin to seek you out. I am often reminded that we are all in that perfect place at all times. I do not believe that anyone can get off their path, though I do think you can sit down in your path and just stew for quite a while. Of course, that allows your suffering to build. We all do it. We say, "I need a break. I've been working awfully hard on this. I need some time for myself." That's the mental self. I believe our path is a winding road. Even with all the mental stuff we do, we cannot stray far from our path.

I recognized I still had a human side within me that was going to play its game and talk me out of all I have gained. Yet, I knew I needed to integrate mindfulness into my quiet ministry. I would take it to work and bring it back on the drive home. I'd continue to work on being centered and mindful from moment to moment. With my feet on the ground and staying aware of my interconnection, I would work on maintaining the expansion that keeps me in the flow with my environment.

All through the time of learning mindfulness, I had a lot of pans in the fire. I was working very hard on my job and self to come to terms with all my new insights. I was a workaholic—I admit it, I love to work. I wasn't able to just sit down, to savor my life. This would be brought back to me later.

I tried to balance my work time and my quest to gain more knowledge through experiences by scheduling in some retreat time. That way I could refill my spiritual cup before it was empty. Taking local classes and attending conferences away from home was a good way to accomplish that. That's how I met Margaret.

Chapter Seven

❀ THE MYSTERY CALLED MARGARET ❀

The joy of all mysteries is the certainty which comes from their contemplation, that there are many doors yet for the soul to open on her upward and inward way.

— *Arthur Christopher Benson*

I was registering at a summer retreat conference in Geneseo, New York when a sweet white-haired older woman came up, hugged me in a very warm embrace, and said brightly, "Hello, David. Welcome," then went on greeting others she knew in the line. Funny, but only Spirit calls me David, not even my mother called me by my proper first name. Even I call myself Dave, and everyone who knows me calls me Dave. I was also astounded that this stranger knew my name when I had not yet picked up my nametag and I was an outsider to this retreat, not well known.

I felt a loving connection with this woman immediately, but didn't really know why. Everyone else waiting to register seemed to know her. After the hug, Spirit suddenly stirred and started speaking to me, telling me to pay attention to this woman. So I asked the person next to me, *"Who is that loving woman?"* I learned her name, Margaret Kean, and that she was teaching a class at the retreat called "Everything You've Always Wanted to Know About Sex and Death." I knew exactly then and there that I had to change my plans and switch into her class.

On the first day I chose to sit in the back to listen to Margaret's lecture. This was a relaxed class—people were sitting on the floor on cushions and chairs were spread in an unorganized fashion. Margaret sat up front with folks all around. To say the room was packed was an understatement. The energy was electric and Spirit was buzzing in my being. Once she started to speak I could see Spirit in her eyes. It was as if I were looking into the Light of Oneness. Shortly into the class I understood why I felt such a strong connection between us: Margaret had had a near-death experience as well! And more surprising, Margaret knew I'd had one, too—she'd seen it in me! She talked directly to me during the class, asking me about my experience, looking to me for comments and confirmations.

Of course, I had not told her I'd had an experience. As a matter of fact, I had not told many people at all. You could count on one hand all the people that knew. Margaret was intent on drawing me out during the class, not allowing me to be the wallflower I intended by sitting way in the back. Her energy was so familiar and loving that I had the urge to divulge parts of my experience I had never shared, though I was still reticent in a class packed full of people.

One evening toward the end of the week I had the opportunity to perform a pipe ceremony with new friends. Pipe always reinforces my connection to the Light, leaving me centered and with my heart wide open. Prayer has that effect on me. Afterward, I went to the common room, and with my heart wide open floated over to Margaret. As she greeted me, I told her, *"Someday I would like to tell you about my near-death experience."* She replied in a sweet but very loud voice, *"I would love to hear your story. Why don't you tell it to us right now?"*

Oh no, I thought, *I did it this time! I'll have to come out from hiding!* This particular spiritual retreat was famous for impromptu rap sessions that often went deep into the night, mostly led by Tom Sawyer. But Margaret's energy was so comforting and calming I couldn't back out; in fact, I wanted to share it all. I began nervously telling my story to Margaret, and soon a group was gathering. Margaret supported me in a loving way, gently nudging me as I struggled to put words to the ineffable. I found it easier to relay my experience talking directly to Margaret and ignoring the others as they listened in. She seemed to allow access to the Light, love and knowledge I had gained from my near death. I felt I could trust her to understand because she too had been there. There was an exchange of loving acceptance from her that reminded me of my Soul Family.

Slowly, more and more people gathered to listen and the room grew quite full as the evening hours dwindled and I shared more than I ever had before. As I was telling my story, I had to open up to the Light, touch it through my heart, and it enveloped me fully. When you are in that place, in God's presence, your false persona is washed away. I could no longer deny my experience or anyone's request to hear it. My heart hurt when I opened up and touched the Light, yet Margaret supported me with a "you can do it, you *have* to do it" look of encouragement. When Margaret looks at you that way, you feel warm and fuzzy, as if you are totally loved and not judged at all. It wasn't like I felt obligated to tell my story for her. I knew that I had to tell my story for myself, and my experience came pouring out. Margaret allowed me to feel safe and know that it is okay to be emotional. I understood then that it would take some time and tissues! to get used to speaking through the emotion and tears. I didn't know it then, but sharing in public was exactly what I needed to move forward with my Purpose.

Margaret is very much like His Holiness the Dalai Lama, an individual who is able to function with an open heart most of the time. When I met her, I realized that this is the most difficult thing anyone could achieve in life. I could not see how I could ever keep my heart open 24/7. We all have to walk around, pay the rent, live our daily lives. I mean we still have to deal with that obnoxious clerk who won't provide a simple service and projects his or her stuff on us. So, it's very difficult to walk this life with your heart open all the time. Although, through Margaret's example it was a goal I wanted to set for myself.

Margaret has her heart wide open about ninety per cent of the time. She is one of the most loving and compassionate people walking this earth. Everyone I've met who knows Margaret feels the same way about being in her presence. They recognize they have experienced unconditional love. She is an amazing teacher and played an integral part of integrating my experience so I could accept it as a part of me.

Doorway Into the Light

Man stands in his own shadow and wonders why it's dark.
— Zen Proverb

After the summer conference, my friend William proposed a trip to visit Margaret at her Smith Mountain Lake home/retreat center in Virginia. He claimed to know the way and was planning on going anyway. At the time, I didn't realize we were not formally invited, information William shared only when we were a few miles from her retreat center.

Margaret lovingly and graciously invited us into her home, though with an odd look. Little did we know at that moment that she had just asked the universe for some help and received instant confirmation from Spirit with us ringing the doorbell.

Margaret headed a healing missionary in Swaziland, Africa. She and her assistant, Libby, spent eight months, or more, of the year bringing medicines and healing to the poor in Africa. Margaret and her husband, Len, had decided to sell the retreat center to allow her more time in Africa. Libby was away drumming up financial support for their upcoming mission work. Hearing all this, William and I immediately offered to help get things ready to sell the property; in exchange Margaret offered guidance, sharing, and her company.

One of the many tasks we tackled was cleaning the stone floor in the front foyer. William and I got down on our hands and knees to scrub it clean. While we were in the process, Margaret walked by and in passing bestowed a gem of wisdom that stays with me to this day: *"How you approach cleaning is the very same way you approach your spirituality."*

Some people clean by starting at one end and work systematically and thoroughly. Others have a scattered approach and hit spots here and there. There is no wrong or right way, only the way we choose. Whatever your cleaning style is, it is more than likely it is going to be the same method you approach your spirituality. There is no wrong or right way, it is just your process. Trained as an engineer, I do things systematically. Mindfulness works well with a systematic approach and my cleaning habits reflect that. Margaret's words not only affirmed my approach to spirituality, it made me realize that you can use cleaning to focus and reflect on your spiritual practice. How cool, another tool!

On one late evening in her living room, Margaret turned to me and asked if I would please share with her the abilities my NDE had given me. I told her about Acceptance, Tolerance, and Truth. I said I could hear Spirit intermittently and am given personal insights that help me in my life, but I confided that I had no control over it. Margaret stopped me there and let me know I could control it if I would just allow it and work with Spirit.

Then she asked me what glimpses of the future I'd had. Until that night, I had never thought to look into the future. Then she asked how often I return into the Light. The thought of returning into the Light was more upsetting to me. I explained how I didn't have the tools to emotionally cope with such an expansive level of love and acceptance. I recounted how my second experience in Sedona had so deeply affected me. Margaret, with her motherly style of insistence and love, told me that returning was something I could do. As we sat there discussing these possibilities, it appeared as if it were only the two of us in the room, which slowly expanded to include the entire universe.

From this place she helped me to go within myself and find the doorway into the Light. Together, we crossed the threshold. While we were there, we were communicating on a totally new level. Again, she asked me to look into the future. With this expansion of consciousness I easily understood the future that was laid out for the people in this country and the world. I saw the financial structure of the country as unstable and the government unable to provide the services we had grown accustomed to. I saw the need for families and communities to come together and support one another. It wasn't the end of the world, or anything that drastic, but needed change in the way we live our lives, changes that were hard for some to comply with. The need for change caused strife for some, but those who were able to go with the flow of change and get involved in a much greater community would be fine. Margaret helped me have my first glimpse into future events. I found out days afterward that William had walked in and saw us "talking without words"—which was the best way he could explain it. The communication was telepathic.

The morning before we left for home, over a breakfast of fresh fruit, we talked about her ability to keep her heart open all the time. She thought our idealistic view of her was amusing and unrealistic. She explained that she gets frustrated like everyone else and there are times she loses patience as well. She tries to filter those times through her heart and not let them get the best of her.

The visit was a quantum leap for me as far as dealing with my near-death experience. Margaret advised me to share it, but to let everyone know that because we'd had an experience it did not make us special. We only have more to live for. I learned from Margaret that whenever an experiencer can share with another experiencer, those are the most liberating and therapeutic times. The other experiencer has been there and there is no need to explain what we can't explain.

I left there with many more tools to employ for my integration, understanding and coping skills. I thank Margaret for showing me that I have the ability to go back into the Light at any time. It is still incredibly emotional, but I know I can do it. Within me was the doorway into the Light, and with her loving support I was able to gingerly touch it. When I am in need I find the doorway within, building new spiritual knowledge that brings even more change in my life. If Richard was the seed of my near-death integration, Margaret was the Miracle Grow that fertilized it! And going back into the Light created the photosynthesis of my growth. I truly started to bring growth home. A lot of my judgments, and that part of my old philosophy that cut my swath through life, slowly melted away. It just isn't a part of who I am anymore. It is much easier to allow life to be.

Margaret Kean passed away the year I was writing this book. The world has lost a shining beacon. She taught many how to live in a mindful manner, and she lives on in the people she touched and loved.

Lessons Gained

We have to create strength where it did not exist before; we have to change our natures, and become new men with new hearts, to be born again.... We need a nucleus of men in whom the Shakti (divine feminine creative power) is developed to its uttermost extent, in whom it fills every corner of the personality and overflows to fertilize the earth.

— *Sri Aurobindo*

With my sudden spurt of spiritual growth I began to change and with that change came some difficult times. Unfortunately, my marriage didn't last. Spirit had been telling me years before that it was time to move on. Suzanne's and my agendas had changed. In the beginning, I chose not to listen to Spirit about this. I fought to keep us together only to end up pushing the relationship further apart. I couldn't ignore it, but eventually I came to accept that Spirit was right and I should allow the change. Emotionally I was not ready to let go, but over time I was able to find release.

Divorce can be a common occurrence after one partner has an NDE. P. M. H. Atwater states in *The Big Book of Near-Death Experiences* that easily 78 per cent of experiencers who were married at the time of their experience end up divorced. I really believe that people come together to learn. Once we learn what we need, it may be time for change. You need to move on to other things.

This period in my life is a good example of how Spirit can talk to me, but I don't always want to listen. We have had some serious debates, Spirit and I. People that know me can tell when this debate is going on; they'll look at me and say, "Dave has zoned out." A relationship with Spirit requires testing in order to trust it. It is a challenge to overcome the doubts that our mind interjects when Spirit says jump. My mind has pushed against Spirit's better judgment, causing some big internal battles. The chattering in my head tries to convince me not to do what Spirit wants: *"You don't need to do that." "You don't have to listen to everything Spirit tells you." "Listen to me. We got along fine before this connection to Spirit when we were cutting our swath through life," "Don't abandon me."* My mind wants equal time.

I found it necessary to balance my time with Spirit and time with my mind. My mind is not a villain, but Spirit helps to keep the mind's role in prospective. I try to keep my mind satisfied. I know I can't live this physical life with only a spiritual connection. That's not why I'm here. I need to experience everything life has to offer in order to evolve. We need the human experience—we can't let the pendulum swing so far to the spiritual side that it denies our human mind. I needed to show my mind that allowing Spirit to speak without being challenged was beneficial. At first the human side needed to learn a little more trust. If I paid attention to Spirit and tried to act when Spirit spoke, the quickening in development and growth would satisfy my mental needs.

Movement on the road to balance, works toward integrating spirit and our human side into one whole being, a universal goal for everyone. I took small steps at first, realizing it is a slow process. Along the road synchronicities are little gifts of confirmation the universe gives to show we are on our path, which is exactly where we need to be.

One method I established to show Spirit I was listening, even if not ready to act, was gratitude. Giving thanks when receiving guidance ensures a continued flow of communication. Gratitude is much more than giving thanks for material things, it is a way of appreciating the gift of life, our experiences, and the guidance we receive. I have found ceremony to be a good way to give thanks and gratitude. If you look at most religious practices they use ceremony to get us to a point where we can take in a spiritual message. Giving the mind something to do helps it to relax and allows Spirit to be heard. Sunday services or reciting mantras are ways to quiet our minds to hear the larger message from Spirit.

The ceremony I use is from the Native American tradition, the pipe ceremony. It is a form of prayer in which you honor and show gratitude to the four cardinal directions of the wind. Each direction represents a part of your own inner nature. Your prayers drift up with the smoke to the four winds with an understanding that your truth will now be known to the world. When ceremony is done in a sacred manner, your mind will allow your heart to speak freely. Once you allow your mind to step aside, these ceremonies become launching points for deeper spiritual connections and reflection. I encourage everyone to find a ceremony that is positive and self-empowering that combines gratitude and a feeling of giving back. Look for ceremonies that are comfortable and follow your own belief system.

The struggle for balance continued in my life. I had times when I forgot to listen, forgot to be compassionate, and forgot to allow love. When I did remember, Spirit was there, loud and clear, to help me continue moving forward on my path. Like Margaret pointed out, we are human and we are fallible.

Eventually I was able to hear Spirit more consistently and I felt comfortable to explore other belief systems. During my explorations I went through a particularly frustrating period when I could not hear Spirit at all. It started when I was looking for Spirit everywhere but within myself. I knew Spirit was love, so anything to do with the topic of love was on my reading list. The urge to find everything there was to know about love became a consuming, voracious compulsion. I read everything I could get my hands on that talked about Love. I even had a cassette to play in the car about finding love. Then, during this searching, I realized I could no longer hear Spirit. Spirit just stopped talking. I was convinced that I was somehow off my path because I couldn't hear Spirit. Fortunately there was another retreat scheduled and I made time to attend. I did everything in my power to study, share and learn with the other people at the retreat, hoping that it would bring me back to my center, my path and I would hear Spirit again.

During a sharing experience at the retreat, Cindy, the woman I'd been partnered with, told me she saw me with a number of white-bellied birds. I didn't know what to make of it; all I knew was that by the end of the weekend, I still hadn't heard a peep from Spirit. After hugs and goodbyes, I shipped off to home. On the drive back, a hawk swooped so close to the front of my van that I thought I was going to hit it. Hawk is a symbol to me that means, *"look around, pay attention"* or *"what was I just thinking?"* In an encounter with a hawk, I look for the special significance to where I am in that moment. I had been thinking about the conference and my quest to hear Spirit as the hawk appeared, so I started to reflect on that. On the hour and a half drive home, I had twelve more close encounters with Hawk. After the thirteenth encounter I heard Spirit, in a jovial way, say, *"Well, now that I have your attention…!"*

I realized that Spirit had never stopped speaking, but I had just stopped listening. This lesson really came home as Spirit showed how I had become so caught up in analyzing love in my mind that I forgot that love is in my heart, love is all of me, love is everything, and love is the Light. I had spent so much time pondering the many views of love in books and how it can turn your life around that I forgot the most important thing: Love is within us at all times and you don't have to go searching for it. It is pure and cannot be damaged or lost. All we need is to open ourselves to love and our true being. When we can achieve that, we experience love for everything and feel the love everything has for us.

Incidentally, when red-tailed hawks swoop by you they show you their white bellies. So of course I had to call Cindy and tell her how the hawks had brought me to look inward. We talked for hours, and though I did not know it then, I had found my true love.

Unconditional Love

The huge concentric waves of universal life are shoreless. The starry sky that we study is but a partial appearance. We grasp but a few meshes of the vast network of existence.

— *Victor Hugo*

Although I had this new way of loving everyone and everything equally, most people didn't see love the same way. Our culture teaches us that the love for a wife or for a child is unconditional. Our minds tell us, however, *"I'm going to love, but I expect love in return."* So there are expectations. Love is not as unconditional as we like to think. There are things we want in return for that love. We do this unconsciously. We have roles we expect others to play, and we will dole out respective levels of love because of our expectations. We're not going to automatically give everyone the whole scoop. We're going to give it out a little at a time, often just a spoonful at a time, because we feel we have to keep some love in reserve. We think, *"It might run out!"* How silly is that? Infinite love can never end.

After my divorce I wanted to develop some new friendships. It was challenging for me because my pendulum had swung so far toward my spiritual side that I was feeling love for everyone and everything. Thus many people misunderstood my loving intention. Women particularly mistook my loving manner as more than friendship, and wanted more serious relationships. Oh boy, was I being naive and blinded by my own spiritual growth. I didn't have a clue about the signals women were sending me! Even when I was honest with them, indicating I was only looking for friendship, they still misinterpreted my loving manner. When I didn't fulfill their expectations, they would get angry. I was really confused! Those monk robes were looking better.

A friend/priest who had experienced a profound spiritual awakening, told me about a book by P. M.H. Atwater, who writes about NDEs, called *Coming Back to Life*. Atwater has interviewed thousands of experiencers. In this book, she is able to categorize a number of the common aftereffects. One thing in it really jumped off the page. She writes that since experiencers have been exposed to the highest level of unconditional love, it changes them and the way they show love.

That's it, my love's changing! I'm not playing the role and I'm not expecting anything in return for the love I'm offering!

I understood that people were expecting me to play the role and I wasn't cooperating. They didn't understand it and until I read the book, neither did I. I knew there was something different about my love, but up until then I couldn't put my finger on it. People around me felt my love going out to everything and they couldn't understand it. Most people still don't understand it, because it is contrary to our normal way of loving. Now that I better understand the power of unconditional love, I try to be aware of how projecting it might be affecting others. Sometimes I find I need to rein it in a little to avoid misunderstandings.

Once I had this realization, it was like a light bulb went off. I had one of those 'Aha' moments. I could see how expectations played roles in my past relationships. When ideas of love and expectations differ, that is when suffering starts. We feel the love is not working. I find it amusing that we often talk about how to "fix" broken love. When and how can love ever be broken? Only possessive or conditional love can be thought of as broken because the expectations of our humanness are not being fulfilled. When our expectations are not met we create our own suffering. Self-imposed suffering is a real physical pain that we feel in our hearts. In order to overcome it we need to clearly examine our expectations.

Interconnection

Do not waste your efforts to win the love of or to fight against friend and foe, children and relatives. See yourself in everyone and give up all feelings of duality completely.

— *Adi Shankara*

I learned in the life review about the interconnection we have to everyone and everything in the universe. Our human nature to need love and to give love creates this interdependence we have with each other. Once you feel this interconnection you cannot help but know compassion for everyone. Compassion leads us to truly care for the well being of any person, regardless of race or background. As compassion grows within so do patience, understanding and tolerance of every situation we experience. With this, love becomes more a state of being instead of something directed toward others. We become a part of the greater love of Oneness and flow with it. The integration of this awareness into our physical being is easy for some and incredibly hard for others. But once integrated, you can begin to open your heart and keep it open longer, projecting more love and compassion.

Working on the importance of love and interconnection, I recall my life review and seeing those ribbons and slivers of light that connect us to one another, how my actions and life experiences affected others. I could see an exchange of energy and communication between us. Many times this is a transfer of communication we are not aware of. This transfer occurs on multiple levels.

Interconnectedness has to do with transfer of energy and communication, one level seems to be on a sub atomic level. Subatomic refers to the electrons and nucleus of atoms. We think of everything as solid and individual. But in a subatomic universe, there is no separateness; there are just slower and faster moving elements. On this level we have protons and electrons that are attracted to each other. We also have the space between the electrons and protons, which plays a part in the attraction and exchange of elements. There is an exchange of elements between everything. Energetically we exchange communication and energy just by being in each other's presence. We also exchange energy through thought and intention. You do not need to be in the same location to have an energy and communication exchange. Also linear time doesn't apply when it comes to interconnection because a past action can create effects at any time. For example, a childhood issue can still affect you as an adult. Fortunately, we can go back and heal past situations and negative energy exchanges.

We may not realize it cognitively, but we are able to sense each other's energy fields. Most of the time we do not consciously recognize what these energies are although some people are sensitive enough to perceive and interpret the energies. We sometimes call this a psychic ability. Our awareness of the communication amplifies the energy and the ability to translate it.

Looking at this interconnection in another way, science has shown us that we are replacing our skin, organs and tissues in an ongoing process. We exhale our cells and breathe in others' cells all the time. Every ten years we are a different person. With this ongoing physical exchange we are all becoming one. I find this amazing; must be the engineer in me.

Understanding interconnection reinforced my goal of becoming more mindful and compassionate. How we live our life and express our emotions affect those around us often without our knowledge. I know I have to take responsibility for my actions and strive to create more peaceful and calm interactions by being more loving. If I changed my output, I could change what I energetically communicate to others. I worked on this by being mindful of my emotions, thoughts and bringing more compassion to my interactions with others. In my life review, it was scary to watch how much energy was projected when my emotions were allowed to go wild. If I bring a more peaceful energy into my being it reduces the rapid, erratic waves of energy exchange, making a smoother, complete communication.

How energy affects others remains a motivation to try and live with an open heart. It's not enough to pray or to meditate about yourself, or to wish for a better life or outcome in a bad situation. That is just being materialistic and self-centered. Rich or poor, a person who lives his or her life with an extraordinary feeling of compassion is someone who has opened their heart. We sometimes let our focus on material things get in the way of opening our hearts and living in a state of love and compassion. Remember, not all spiritual men and women wear robes or live a monastic life. Balancing enough materialism to support your spiritual side is a way to a healthy and compassionate life. Everything is love, and it is through living compassionately that we will have everything we need.

Spirit started conveying that I needed to prepare for change. I knew that my role in the dialysis centers was coming to an end, but it wasn't clear where I should go from here. *Am I going to move to another area? Am I going to change career paths again?*

Spirit communicated to me that I needed to schedule a vacation and gave me the specific dates. Even though I was the manager of my department, I still needed to get permission to take time off. By now everyone at work knew that whenever I took vacation time, I did something unusual. So I kept getting asked by coworkers, "What adventure do you have planned this time?" I didn't have any answers for them. When I questioned Spirit, the only response I received was that I would be heading to the coast. Living in central New York State, I assumed that meant going east, toward Connecticut or New York City. My director had already approved the dates so I waited for more direction.

Weeks before my scheduled time off, my friend Cindy Griffith called me. She asked if I wanted to join her and another friend Christopher for three days as

American students with His Holiness, the Dalai Lama. He was going to be at the Chuang-Yen Monastery in Kent, New York, to dedicate the great Buddha Hall and give teachings on the way of the bodhisattva. When Cindy gave me the dates of May 25–27, I had to laugh.

Now I knew where I was going on my vacation! I thanked the universe for this phenomenal gift, which had shown me that I was exactly where I needed to be. This might well be the first step in preparation for the changes that Spirit kept predicting.

Chapter Eight

❀ LIVING EULOGY ❀

And after your death, when most of you for the first time realize what life here is all about, you will begin to see that your life here is almost nothing but the sum total of every choice you have made during every moment of your life. Your thoughts, which you are responsible for, are as real as your deeds. You will begin to realize that every word and every deed affects your life and has also touched thousands of lives.

— *Elisabeth Kubler-Ross*

In November of 2000 my life was starting to smooth out again. In the past three years, I had surrounded myself with people I could open up to—and my relationship with Cindy was blooming! Yet I had chronic pain in my neck and arm. I also had an annoying crick in my back. I didn't give these symptoms a lot of thought because I figured it was carpal tunnel syndrome from all the computer work I was doing for the dialysis program at St. Joseph's Hospital. Then one day I was in my office and suddenly felt as though my back had exploded. The pain was so great it brought tears to my eyes. Being in pain, and not thinking clearly, I tottered into my director's office, interrupting a meeting. I bluntly informed her that I was going to the emergency room. As I walked two blocks uphill to the hospital's emergency department, all I could see was a throbbing red haze.

When I arrived at the emergency department, they recognized me as a manager of the dialysis program, so I didn't have to wait for triage. I explained the symptoms of severe pain in my back and numbness in my arm. They immediately assumed it was a heart attack, put me on a gurney and attached a 12-lead EKG. I kept trying to tell them no, it's not a cardiac arrest—I just needed pain medication and x-rays of my back. I only wanted them to stop the pain please, please stop the pain! After a very long observation, they ruled out cardiac arrest. Okay, I understood they had their protocols. They have to do their own thing. I had learned the lesson about each of us having our own path. I also had my own path, and unfortunately right now ours were not in sync.

Finally, after what seemed like hours, they decided to send me for x-rays. But they still wouldn't give me any pain medicine. Over the years I had learned I had a high tolerance to pain, but this was way beyond any pain I had experienced, even the pain of death! The x-ray technician informed me that he was going to do a full series. He had me on the table twisting my body one way and then another. Then he had me standing up. He even made me stand holding 20-pound (10kg) sandbags at my sides. Well, that caused the pain to be so excruciating that tears poured down my face and the sandbags almost sent me to my knees. I kept asking them to hurry: *"Please take the shot and let get me out of here!" "Would someone please give me some pain medicine?"* No. They returned me to the ED where I then waited in my room for quite a while.

I called Cindy, who arrived before the doctors returned. I told her I had been in the ED all day and was experiencing so much pain that I didn't think I was going to be able to go home tonight. Of course, she was a little upset because I hadn't called her sooner. I lay on the gurney feeling frustrated and not in control. Cindy was going back and forth between angry and worried. Betty, the nurse assigned to my case, had worked for me as a secretary while she was going to nursing school, so I was getting the best care and a lot of attention. I felt quite privileged, like a VIP, but still no darned pain medication. When the doctor came in he was shuffling his feet, hemming and hawing and trying not to look at me. He kept saying "Well Dave…" over and over. My nurse had tears in her eyes. Cindy and I were mute, just watching the show and waiting.

At that moment I realized I had seen all this before. I had seen it happen in my life review. I actually smiled as I watched the doctor and his discomfort at having to tell me about the massive tumors that were in my lung and spine. I let him struggle—I probably won't be proud of that moment in my next life review. He wanted to keep me for more tests, because he needed to take a good, long, hard look at this and get it correct. Of course doctors and medical professionals don't use the C-word. They don't call it cancer to your face. They say something like, "You have some masses we would like to investigate." Finally, they gave me the pain medication and I was shipped to the oncology floor, exhausted from fighting the pain all day long.

I accepted the cancer news immediately. I had no problem with the diagnosis because I had already seen myself dealing with cancer in my life review. I also knew I was going to be okay, because I saw myself living beyond the cancer. The next morning the test started. They kept me in the hospital, performing every test available utilizing the latest technology, and bombarding my body, for a week and a half. Finally results started coming in. The cancer had started in my right lung and had metastasized outward, eating three bones in my spine. Finally, my spine had collapsed because the T2 thoracic bone was no longer there and the tumor could not support the weight. No wonder I was in pain: I had a broken back. They found lesions in my brain, hip, and kidney. A spine surgeon was asked to consult on my case but after studying my voluminous chart he told me it wasn't worth considering spine surgery because I probably had less than eight weeks to survive. *Wow*, I thought, *That's a tough prognosis.*

During my time in the hospital I experienced some incredibly humbling events. The oncology floor nurses had to stop well-wishers from visiting so that I could get some rest. A steady crowd of people I knew came by day and night. Because hospitals are open twenty-four hours a day, seven days a week, I had gotten to know people on every shift. Even some of the hospital maintenance guys came by, making an excuse to come fix something on my floor then spending the time with me. I did like seeing everyone, especially my friends and coworkers, and even my bosses, the hospital president and vice presidents stopped by.

I have come to think of these visits as my third life review. Almost everyone I knew, even people I didn't supervise, stopped by and gave testimony or the equivalent of a eulogy as to how I had affected them in their lives. I'd say, *"Oh please, don't tell me this stuff or compliment me that way. You're making me cry!"* (I am not the type of person who receives compliments well. It's one of my issues in this life, and I have been working on it, though unsuccessfully.) The next person waiting at the door would listen to the first person's stories, and it went on and on like that. It was amazingly humbling because I knew I wasn't going to die. I kept trying to tell my visitors that, but no one would listen. So I found myself consoling these people who were going through stages of grief over my loss. That's a funny way to phrase it when you think about it, *grief over my loss*. They thought they were going to lose me. But I had total faith in what I had experienced in my life review, which had shown me I was going to get through this.

Many are familiar with Elisabeth Kubler-Ross's five stages of grieving. The first stage is denial. After that you go through anger, bargaining, and depression—and then you finally reach acceptance. Since I had already observed my cancer in my life review, I didn't go through the typical grieving process. When I got the news in the emergency room, it was old news to me. Although everyone misunderstood my optimism and positive attitude as stage one of denial, in reality I was already in stage five, acceptance. Everyone, and I mean everyone, thought I was in denial and about to die.

When cancer is first diagnosed in a person the first fear most folks have is: *"Am I going to die?"* This is the normal overwhelming first thought and often leaves no room for any other thought or emotion. The first few weeks the person will be in a fog and they may not realize it; thinking will be cloudy and concentration difficult. It may seem like the person is zoning out. But the diagnosis will usually shock the person into some sort of action. The action may be positive or negative, but either way it marks the beginning of that person's future path and heightened insight on what is important in his or her life.

I was fortunate enough to not have the fear of death, an after effect of my NDE. I have to admit the temptation was there to not move forward, not to treat the cancer and to allow myself to go home to the Light. I even attempted to try to push Cindy away because I didn't want her to suffer through my hardship. But I ultimately realized that I was stronger accepting her help. I knew that there were experiences in the cancer treatments and in living life afterward that I needed to complete. I understood the potential to grow and learn about myself and the strength gained by overcoming such huge obstacles.

As I was experiencing my positive insights about starting my cancer treatments, in the next room a man was in the final stages of cancer. His family was very upset and did not want him to die. They told him this over and over. Many times I observed their fears in the hallway. Their fears were revealed in wailing, crying and loud discussions as I was wheeled in and out of my room. Through the walls I could feel the man's anguish and torment at leaving his family and the weariness of his soul from fighting the cancer. In the quiet early hours before dawn I found myself in his room consoling him and telling him there is nothing to fear in death. I was not physically in his room, but my consciousness was. While practicing my mindfulness my expanded consciousness was able to visit him and give support. One morning he at last let go and passed into the Light with what I perceived as a smile and a wave goodbye.

Pain, Pain, Go Away

When the senses contact sense objects, a person experiences cold or heat, pleasure or pain. These experiences are fleeting; they come and go. Bear them patiently.

— *The Bhagavad Gita*

The crick in my back before the diagnosis was probably the tumor. Before everything went south with my spine I didn't know I was so sick. I was not feeling the lung cancer, but I had to deal with extreme pain from my collapsed spine. At first we didn't know how to treat the pain without overmedicating me. Every time a medical staff member came in to check on me or take me for another test, I'd always be asked about my pain level. It seemed as though the knee-jerk reaction was to instantly medicate me, which created a morphine and Percocet roller coaster. I was high as a kite one moment, then back to extreme agony when the drugs wore off.

Every time my pain increased my blood pressure and pulse would go up, and up. They gave me more pain meds, but these took a while to work. One morning, awaiting my pain medication, Spirit spoke to me and gave me a visualization to manage my pain. I used Spirit's visualization to change the pain into love and compassion, giving the medications a chance to work. This helped a great deal to lower my blood pressure and allowed me to relax and breathe.

These were Spirit's instructions:

- Give thanks for this life. Honor and be grateful for the aspects that have the greatest meaning in your life (Love, Truth, Acceptance, Compassion, Tolerance and Respect. I used my daily gratitude prayer for this). Then, take a few minutes to relax and find your meditative state.
- Visualize your heart as a rosebud that is starting to bloom. Slowly the petals grow longer and ever so slowly they start to glow with a pure white light. As the flower starts to open it becomes brighter with the Light of pure love and compassion.
- Feel the warmth from the love and compassion growing through your heart. After a while all that remains will be brilliant pure Light. Slowly begin to expand the Light to the rest of your body. Once the Light has enveloped your body, expand the Light from the base of your spine to Mother Earth, and feel that connection. Next, expand from the top of your crown to Father Sky and again feel the connection.
- Take time to feel your body being bathed in this warm light of love and compassion. Locate your pain and wrap your pain or suffering with the Light. Visualize the pain and suffering being transformed or converted into love and compassion. Allow it to dissolve away until only the light of love and compassion is left.
- Now raise the Light up through your crown to Father Sky and release the pain and suffering, transmuted into love and compassion, onto the winds of the universe. Then slowly come back to your body and where you physically are.

With Spirit's visualization and the proper medication for the pain, I felt fine. From then on it was the cancer treatment that hurt and caused much of the distress. The medical treatments for cancer are still pretty rough, as though we're still in the era of the caveman. I've always wanted something like the pill Dr. McCoy gave the woman in *Star Trek*, to help her grow her kidney back. My cancer treatments were far worse than the disease.

Medical Team

Life is given to us on the definite understanding that we boldly defend it to the last.

— *Charles Dickens*

For people unfamiliar with the medical profession, all this contact with medical persons, however welcome, can tie up much of the mental and emotional energy you have when you're in treatment. I recommend making lists of questions for your meetings with doctors. Bring someone with you to take notes, because your mental fog will make it difficult for you to absorb the information you are looking for. The doctor may counsel about one thing, your mind will get stuck on that element while the doctor keeps going and you miss half of what is said. Remember, two heads are always better than one, so don't be afraid that it might be a burden to tell the friend/loved one who is taking notes what information you need.

I used my intuitive skills and listening to Spirit to pick my care team and choose my treatment options. To get past the cancer, I realized I had my part to play in my healing, and I took that role very seriously. Working at the hospital helped. Because I knew the medical community, I was fortunate to be able to pick some of the best doctors in our area. I communicated what I felt I needed to this health care team. I asked them to be open and honest with me as well. I let them know that if they didn't want to work with me, I would go to someone else. (Needless to say, the spine surgeon who didn't think I would make it was let go.)

Together, my care team and I chose a very aggressive treatment plan. After a couple of weeks in the hospital I was discharged. My radiation and chemo treatments were prescribed and the first treatments were completed. Cindy was away working, so a wonderful friend, Julie Bourbon, got me home after being discharged with a prescription for pain medications that my home pharmacy couldn't fill. She fought like a tiger so I could get what I needed. She was the right person at the right time to deal with the situation; she is a medical social worker. This was more confirmation that I was where I needed to be.

Treatments

All strength, all healing of every nature is the changing of the vibrations from within, the attuning of the divine within the living tissue of a body to Creative Energies. This alone is healing.

— *Edgar Cayce*

I continued chemotherapy and radiation as an outpatient for months. The fact that I had radiation and chemo at the same time shows how aggressive our approach was. I balanced hospital treatment out with holistic methods. Cindy and I realized that we needed to get the word out about my situation. Sharing all life experiences is the way to living with your truth. By doing this, unexpected support came back for both of us. Friends and family offered us many types of holistic remedies for cancer.

Considering that there are so many different types of cancer and everyone's body is different, I found I had to listen to my heart to find which remedies would work best with my body and illness. (A word of caution here—what I used is not going to work for everyone. We all need to use our own guidance to determine what will work best for us.) I used a nutritional supplement developed to help my digestive system because eating was so incredibly difficult. I drank essiac tea and took reishi mushrooms daily for my weakened immune system and to boost the antioxidants in my body.

Along with suggestions for remedies came many, many prayers. I soundly believe in the healing power of prayer and strongly support getting the word out so prayer groups can participate. Cindy's mother, who did not live in our area, felt as if there was nothing she or other family members could do from a distance. So, she spoke to her pastor about it. He suggested that she put together a prayer blanket. Friends and family would pray while they were knitting the squares and she would pray as she put them together. This is a wonderful way to be active in someone's healing if you are not nearby. Having something positive to do also kept her worry in check. The answer to the call for prayer squares was so great that she made a blanket and a shawl. It is unclear if the chemo or the radiation caused me to be cold most of the time, but the warmth of these gifts was more than welcome. When I put the shawl around me I could feel the love and found it calming and soothing. Feeling those prayers reminded me of the slivers of interconnected light I saw in my NDE. Spirit showed me that using the focus of our prayers is a wonderful way to initiate that transfer of light between us.

For seven weeks I went for radiation treatments every day, Monday through Friday. All the radiation staff were wonderful. Part of the procedure required them to tattoo some alignment marks on my chest and make a body cast so that each time I came for treatment I would be perfectly aligned with the equipment as I lay on the table. They also drew lines on my chest with Sharpie permanent markers to highlight the tiny tattoos. We joked around so much that sometimes a little smiley face appeared on my belly or shoulder. Some of those techs were pretty good artists! All this lifted my spirits during a very trying and painful time. Lying there with my hands over my head with a broken spine was excruciating.

The staff never forgot that I was in a lot of pain or that the equipment could be intimidating. I found it helpful to understand the way the radiation machines worked on my body. With my background in dialysis, I was accustomed to working with medical equipment, and the techs took the time to answer any questions I had about the radiation equipment as they prepared me for treatment. The setup was usually longer than the treatment.

Spirit was insisting that I visualize the tumor. Feeling that a picture is worth a thousand words, I asked the technician to show me my tumor from the CAT scan. My job in my healing process started when the technicians left the room. Once the machine started buzzing and clicking, I visualized the mass in my body. I saw the radiation energy as a feather brushing up against the mass, slowly wearing it down. I was allowed to have my *malas* (prayer beads) wrapped around my wrist and hand and I would use them in my visualizations. After seeing the x-ray film, I realized that my tumor was quite large, and if I shrank it too fast or all at once, it would create a void within me. I was concerned that my body might react in distress if the tumor was reduced too fast. Being realistic, Spirit and I visualized shrinking the mass a little at a time, with love in my heart.

Dr. Dalope, my radiation oncologist, is a very loving doctor who isn't afraid to get close to his patients. To give us hope, he told us about his one patient who had survived cancer even worse than mine. Cindy and I asked each other later, *"There was only one?"* For my chemo treatments I went to another oncologist, Dr. Santo DiFino. We had an incredible amount of confidence in Dr. DiFino and his staff and were impressed at how much respect and compassion they showed patients and their families. There was always an extra chair beside me in the exam room for Cindy. They also made the environment as comfortable as possible with TV, video, drinks, books and calming murals on the walls. My weekly chemo treatments consisted of three hours of infusion. When my radiation treatments were completed, Dr. DiFino then scheduled six-hour chemo infusions with multiple chemo drugs every three weeks.

When you begin a fight against cancer you struggle to keep the sense of control you are used to having. But total control during cancer treatment is not possible. Once you give up trying to control everything, you'll start seeing aspects of your body, mind, and relationships in a new way. Personal priorities become clearer or heightened. Many cancer survivors consider this heightened insight a positive result of their cancer experience. The process of letting go opens new doors to self-understanding.

Letting go also helps when experiencing the frustration that results from the treatments. The longer a person is having treatment the more opportunity for frustration coming into play. When loss of physical control and fatigue is keeping you from what you want, then you need to also let go of pushing your physical limits. I often speak about fighting the fatigue, but you also need to know your limits. When you really want to do something, then do as much you can in smaller steps. This helps to keep a good sense of your self-worth and belief in your abilities.

The first treatment will change the cycle and rhythms you are accustomed to. I found that learning this new rhythm helped me to go with the flow of the treatments. Remember the mental fog? It may take a couple of treatments to really understand these new cycles. It is important to note that most cancer treatments are cumulative, so the aftereffects get worse with each treatment. When you understand your cycles then you can attend to the job at hand and do your part in healing. You can start to schedule your life's needs around the new life/treatment rhythms. Recognize that there are going to be bad days and good days. On the bad days do not schedule anything; you may not even want to communicate. But on the good days you will be more apt to be active and responsive to suggestions. That is when fighting the fatigue is possible.

Cancer patients can be amazed at how resilient the human body can be. It helps to understand that the more you allow the strength of your body to work with the treatment, the more successful your treatment will be. If you don't waste energy fighting the treatment, you will have more energy to listen and work with the new clearer insights your connection to your true being will have, and to heal.

Loss of Job

Bereavement is the deepest initiation into the mysteries of human life, an initiation more searching and profound than even happy love... Bereavement is the sharpest challenge to trust in God: if faith can overcome this, there is no mountain which it cannot remove.
— *William Ralph Inge*

During one of my first chemo treatments, I received a visit from the social worker assigned to my case. I figured this was a formality, to see how I was getting along financially and emotionally. Instead, she started by asking me how was I going to support myself. I was planning on returning to work in a few months—I had plenty of sick time banked. Retirement had never crossed my mind, however, I was now being clearly told by this woman that I was never going to be able to work again. She said I would need at least six months of treatment and then probably another six-month run living with a collapsed spine. When she realized I was not comprehending any of this, she took a step back and explained more about the treatments ahead of me and that returning to work would not be possible.

I went into shock. It was very hard to face the loss of my job. I am a workaholic, have been all my life—I enjoy working. Suddenly I had to face the reality that at the age of forty-five I could be 100 percent disabled. Treatments might last six months to a year or more just to fight stage IV lung cancer and get it into remission. At that point it will still be considered incurable. Doctors said I might get to live a year or two: "Make the best of it while you can, retire." I needed to look at this situation one step at a time. I realized that I was no longer going to be this guy who went to work each day. I had put fifteen years into the dialysis program and was very proud of what I had accomplished. To give up that kind of dedication required undergoing major mental housekeeping. I had to let go of a lot and transfer all the details I had in my head to someone else, a huge undertaking.

Most of us use our creativity in the workplace. When you create you are bringing something to life. To lose what you create results in a feeling of great emptiness. Our culture teaches us that our job is a part of our identity. I had to grieve for the loss of my employment, like the death of a loved one. Not having a job decreases our self-worth. Once I got over the shock of losing this part of myself, I realized that I had to make my healing process my new job.

Cindy and I decided that our plan was for me to live for ten years or more. From then on whenever someone started to speak in a negative way about my prognosis, we would say that we were on the "Ten-Year Plan."

Chapter Nine

❈ THE COURSE TO HEALING ❈

The wise man is as a guest-house, and he admits all the thoughts that occur to him, whether of joy or of sorrow, with the same welcome, knowing that like Abraham, he may entertain angels unawares.

— Rumi

I start all my spiritual practices with my gratitude prayer. It could be said I perform that rite at the drop of a hat. We find ceremony in all faiths, religions, and philosophies. If you take the Eucharist, that is a ceremony. We put ceremony in many of our life's gatherings; it's seen everywhere. Even at the beginning of sports events we sing the national anthem. Ceremonies are so integrated into our culture we don't even recognize them as such. We just go through the motions of what is expected from us. Wouldn't it be something special if we could give ceremonies the reverence they were originally intended to have?

I have found that adding a small ritual before meditating gives my mind something to do and helps make my mind quieter. Ceremonies do not have to be long and elaborate, although large is pleasant as well. I realized soon after my diagnosis that I needed to put some rituals into my healing process.

People ask me how I was able to introduce ceremony into my treatment. I set up a little altar on my side table with a medicine Buddha, my malas, and a medicine wheel I'd made for myself. As soon as the chemo bags came up from the pharmacy and before the nursing staff connected them, I would ask to say a prayer and blessing over the bags. The staff had no trouble with my participation in my healing. As a matter of fact, they were understanding and supportive. My intent was to invite the Universal Consciousness to integrate with my chemo chemical cocktail, permeating it with conscious energy so the treatment could work with the highest intention and purest manner in my body, with love, light, and the hope that my healing would be for the highest good. My treatment prayer helped me to cope with, and made it easer to go through, the chemical infusions. I could feel the drugs attacking my body's cells, so the intention of it being for the highest good was vital. Sometimes

I would include a meditation or visualization to ease my suffering. These actions allowed my human side to release and accept the healing process.

Visualizations and meditations are ceremonies that calm and quiet my human side. *"I am grateful for…, I purify myself for…, I give thanks for…"* All of these are intended for the entire body, mind, and spirit. They calm and strengthen us and allow the healing to continue.

Gratitude Prayer

Gratitude bestows reverence, allowing us to encounter everyday epiphanies, those transcendent moments of awe that change forever how we experience life and the world.

— *John Milton*

I applied what I learned about gratitude in pipe ceremonies and expanded it to be part of my healing process. Our true being (body, mind and spirit) benefits by being grateful for all aspects of our lives. Somewhere along the way we have forgotten to give praise every day. Simply look at nature for inspiration: listen to the birds; you hear their songs praising the morning dawn and again singing toward the end of daylight. Praise is a gateway into giving something back, specifically, returning your energy into the universal consciousness.

So what do you put in a gratitude prayer? Each one of us has something to be grateful for. I am a pipe holder so my personal prayer has a Native American flavor to it. A daily prayer comes from your heart. It will give you strength every time you acknowledge your gratitude. Pick out a few aspects of your life, like love, acceptance, tolerance, sharing, truth, and respect. Your daily praise should start small and build over time. I've found it takes on a guidance of its own. Your heart will speak your truth into your praise. Make it personal at first, until it feels comfortable, and then expand it to include family and friends. For those of you who are practicing mindfulness, gratitude is a great way to start the day, connect, and return to your center when you are pulled off it. Tie the prayer into your spiritual beliefs. Give thanks for your life to God, Goddess, or All That Is.

Gratitude is a major tool in healing. After a spiritual ceremony you will find that your pulse rate drops and you are more relaxed. Being in that state of relaxation increases the ability of your physical body to heal and accept treatment. This is another sign of the balance we need to be looking for and maintaining during any healing process.

Many friends and family members couldn't understand how I could be *grateful* while I was going through all this pain. What was there to be grateful for, they wondered. My two NDEs taught me to cherish all experiences, and by expressing my gratitude, I take the time to look at and get the most out of all experiences. I don't look at them as good or bad. I try not to judge daily occurrences. It was clear to me that these incredibly difficult treatments and the long suffering afterward were somehow an important part of my purpose. Knowing that, how could I NOT be grateful? As bad as my health and pain was, I always met someone in the treatment areas who was going through even tougher times. So I made sure to include those less fortunate in my prayers.

When do I make my gratitude prayers? I enjoy giving praise like the songbirds, first thing in the morning before I even put my feet on the floor. I also enjoy sunset or any time that something touches my heart or spirit. A simple traditional gratitude prayer can be at mealtime: *"Thank you for the food being received, where it came from and those who helped to bring it."* Being grateful is the first step in prayer, meditation, and ceremony.

Every path has a few stones or obstacles to overcome. Praise can be very hard to find in today's culture, where no one has time and everything feels like it's going at breakneck speed. Daily prayer and praise can help overcome any obstacles by identifying and understanding them, rather than judging them.

Prayer does not have to be long or elaborate. Prayer doesn't have to be religious; it is simply a way to communicate your truth to the Universal All. I pray anywhere I feel comfortable. I enjoy nature elements so I like nature around me whenever I'm praying or praising, especially if that occurs when problem solving or planning. If you can't go out and build a campfire for your daily prayer session, I recommend lighting a candle instead. Create a special place in your home, maybe just a shelf for an altar, as a sacred place to connect. Or how about the shower? That's private, I especially like it because the natural elements of heat and water are represented and I don't have to schedule extra or special time.

How much time do we spend alone in the car? Spirit loves to communicate in the car for some reason. I suspect the mind is busy driving and Spirit sees an opening. We have more opportunities than we think. When I am having trouble sleeping, a gratitude prayer can help me relax and release. If I have a full day ahead, praise can help me de-stress and be more on track and focused. Gratitude prayers and praise are really good anytime I want to realign and become balanced.

                                     ॐ   ॐ

My dearest friend, companion, and now my wife, Cindy, once wrote an article called *"Keep It Simple Spiritually (K.I.S.S.)"* and that is the way we should approach healing terminal illness. A part of healing illness is balance. Everything in our material universe is seeking balance all the way down to the atomic level. One key part of balance that most of us forget is the need to give back. If we are receiving healing energy then we need to return a positive energy. Giving back can be as simple as sharing your enlightenment and Spirit with others at any opportunity that comes along. You do not have to give away large monetary amounts, even though charity is good. I try to give back something on Twitter and Facebook everyday. To really effect change in this world you need to reach out to others with greater understanding and remember the interconnectedness between us all. When you can do this greater acceptance and tolerance will come. Then you can grow more universal love and compassion for others.

Reaching out with an open heart is the most wonderful gift you can give. To face your own mortality you have to face your own heart. If shared with others, the truth that lives within your heart will touch and stay with them. Your heart becomes a part of their lives and then becomes a part of their quiet ministries. You and your essence of who you are never go away. Who you are becomes a part of everyone you've touched. So again, in order to heal and have the coping skills needed to deal with cancer or any terminal illness, you must find ways of giving back to achieve balance.

When working with your connection to Spirit and increasing our spiritual growth, you must not forget the self, body and mind. Foster the positive aspects of your human side at the same time as you grow spiritually. In my healing process, balance is the most important part of my work—I have to keep the life force energy flowing in order to heal. How do you foster your human side? What do you do? I've already discussed prayer and visualization as excellent ways of fulfilling that need. These practices allow the human side to release the suffering and build up positive life force at the same time. Strengthen your truth, compassion, love, humor, your drive, and self-esteem, which are all things that make us human and allow us to share our heart with others. Meanwhile Spirit can work on amplifying our connection to our true being so the spiritual healing energies can flow in a more natural rhythm.

Even though I was grateful for the experiences, I still had to deal with the constant daily pain of a collapsed spine on top of the cancer treatments. The doctors at the hospital, who were very concerned that I avoid severe pain, sent me home with a pint (half litre) of morphine, a bottle of Percocet, and told me to manage my pain. I'd let them know that a little pain is okay as long as I retained my clarity. I did not want to be in a total fog all the time. I needed to be lucid; otherwise my quality of life suffered. They respected that, but stressed that there is no reason why anyone should have to suffer with pain. I could acknowledge their wisdom because I saw how pain would distract from mindfulness and healing. Through observation they saw that I was not abusing my pain medications and was not unduly suffering from pain; they gave me carte blanche on medications.

To further manage my chronic pain, I also had to learn how the chemo and radiation treatments affected me. I examined the cycles my body went through as a result of each type of treatment. Each medication they gave me had different effects and cycles. I asked the medical staff to explain how each medication differed in how it delivered pain relief and in what duration. Some drugs worked fast with a short life span while others took longer to kick in but were better for long-term pain management. Sometimes I needed to switch drugs because I was too foggy. At first the fog disturbed me because with all the medications I was on I couldn't hear Spirit. I finally realized that I needed the pain medications to cope with my daily activities. But if I started to dose down in the afternoon, then by the middle of the night the medication would wear off enough and I could have lucid conversations with Spirit in what I called the Hour of the Wolf.

Around 3:33 each morning, Wolf would usually present himself in my dreams. I'd wake up to a quiet house and go into our meditation room. Once I had settled in I began with a meditation, then Spirit and I would converse and visit. I quietly spoke into a voice-activated tape recorder, repeating what Spirit was lovingly sharing. I felt relieved once we started having these wonderful conversations. Many contained instructions that showed me how to overcome the pain and become cancer-free. The joy I experienced during these early morning meetings gave me the strength to continue another day. At last, I'd found a way to overcome the fog.

Visualizations

All men wondered to see the water turned into wine. Everyday the earth's moisture being drawn into root of a vine, is turned by the grape into wine, and no man wonders. Full of wonder then are all the things, which men never think to wonder at.

— Pope St. Gregory

Months prior to my cancer diagnosis, Cindy and I had moved to Tully, New York. We'd found a beautiful place to live, high up on the side of a hill in what used to be a cross-country ski resort. The spectacular view, the sense of peace and tranquility were what really drew us there. We had an extra bedroom and took great pains to create the perfect meditation room. We had Tibetan Buddhist thangkas on the wall, meditation cushions, artwork, and beautiful altars. We really spent a lot of time and effort to create an inspirational environment. Yet our lifestyles were so hectic before I became sick, we'd never had time to enjoy our meditation room.

Now, thanks to Wolf, I was often in the ready-made healing meditation room to make my connection to the Light. This incredible night-time focus brought all of the gifts from the first near-death experience along with the acceptance of the second experience into a new clarity. I received insights and visualizations that, amazingly, helped me relieve my pain and suffering. I also spent a couple hours in the room each early morning recharging, spiritually refilling my cup. It gave me the strength to start another day as well as the confirmation that I was right where I needed to be and doing what I was supposed to do.

Visualization and meditation are disciplines that work on many levels to help calm our human selves and allow Spirit to give the insights needed to stay positive in healing, overcoming cancer or any struggle we might be experiencing. If you haven't meditated before, start out slowly. Meditation is an individual process for each of us, so use the following exercises only if they feel right for you. I used these visualizations during my healing, but they can be used for anything troubling you. Perform the visualizations step by step. You might want to record the steps on a recorder and play it back the first few times until you're comfortable with the process. Add or subtract steps or words, as you feel guided.

Cancer Healing Visualization

- Take slow relaxing breaths. Slowly breathe in, thinking Calm, and then slowly breathe out your stress. Perform as many breaths as you need to feel relaxed. In order to calm your mind and your human self, be grateful and give thanks for where you are as well as all the support you have been given. Take as much time as needed to include everything and everyone.
- Then try forgiving all the real and imagined wrongs that have hurt you.
- Visualize all the negative thoughts and fears about your illness as a dark color. See the darkness from the pain and suffering from the disease being pulled up and out of the body. Continue with this until you feel yourself relaxing, going deeper into a meditative state.
- Be mindful as you breathe: breathe in Comfort, and then breathe out your tension.
- Visualize your heart radiating a white and gold light. From this light come millions of smaller light bubbles that are being sent out to dissolve the dark cancer cells, negative thoughts, and fears. The light bubbles transform them into Love and Light.

- Then release this Love and Light back into the universe out of the top of your head and onto the four winds.
- While continuing breathing mindfully, visualize your heart as a green color. Pick a color green that brings you comfort. Send the green light bubbles to heal the damaged cells left after the treatment. This is necessary to create balance in your body.
- Return your heart's light to the white and gold light. Now send it through the body for courage and strength. Breathe in Courage and breathe out Strength.
- Slowly expand this light outside your physical body to form a shield or bubble of strength. Allow yourself to sit with this for a moment so your body can remember the feeling afterward, leaving an indelible imprint.
- Allow yourself to return, feeling your feet, legs, torso, arms and head.

Allowing Spirit to Speak Visualization

I realize not everyone can hear Spirit. During one of my early morning conversations, I received a meditation to share so others can hear Spirit. The visualization starts with an understanding of our relationship to the elements. I am sharing with you the abstract concept of this meditation the same way I heard it from Spirit:

"Most people require hearing and reminding that you are human. You are made up from the earth's elements. There is a call to be grateful for that, because you live here and walk on Mother Earth and she is a limited resource. You need to give thanks for what you take from the Mother. What you take into your bodies, your fuel, comes from the earth element, the Mother. The element of air that you breathe gives you your life, your breath. It gives oxygen to your blood that runs through your body and that oxygenated blood gives you your power. It helps to cleanse and enrich your tissues. The water in your body flows through every part of you and gives you your energy, your chi. The fire element is in your heart, it is your spirit and your love that is the element of fire. A simple visualization to remind you that your body and the elements are related can be helpful."

In order to hear Spirit you have to tell your mind to allow Spirit to speak. You can do it with this visualization:

- Imagine yourself as flowing water, picturing this as the waters of your life.
- Next imagine releasing control of your mind onto the waters of your life. Allow your mind and the waters to flow freely together. Release your mind to the waters, to your flow.
- The fire and love of your heart causes the flow of life to become brighter. As it flows from your mind through your heart, it becomes pure light.

- Allow your flow of life to remain in this light and dwell within it.
- Allow the light to expand, moving outward in all directions.
- Allow this light to flow and encompass your entire body.
- Then allow it to become one with its surroundings.
- Allow it to feel and touch Mother Earth and let it feel the winds of Father Sky.
- Now allow Spirit to speak to you.
- Take in what knowledge Spirit gives you, continue allowing your self to dwell in the light, and keep the flow open.
- When Spirit speaks to you remember to give thanks in return.
- Then slowly allow yourself to come back, back to your heart. Feel the flow of life energy in your body.
- Let yourself come back to your mind and body, back to your physical surroundings.

Use this visualization to allow Spirit to converse with you. *Allowing* is key, and though it sounds very simple, if you live life in your mind, as I did before my experiences, then it is difficult to break out of the pattern. This simple visualization can help you form a new pattern of allowing Spirit communication in addition to normal thinking. When you're done, don't analyze what you have received in the visualization, accept it. That way it becomes a part of you and connected to the universal All.

The snow started falling on our quiet healing retreat in the hills of upstate New York, showing us the beauty of winter and the wonder of the Christmas season. But when it came time to make the trips to the treatment center the roads were always passable and we were never delayed due to the weather. This served as another reminder that I was on track in my voyage toward serving my purpose.

Chapter Ten

❊ THE CHRISTMAS MIRACLE ❊

God hath placed by the side of each man his own Guardian Spirit,
who is charged to watch over him — a Guardian who sleeps not nor
is deceived. For to what better or more watchful Guardian could He
have committed each of us? So when you have shut the doors and
made a darkness within, remember never to say that you are alone;
for you are not alone, but God is within, and your Guardian Spirit,
and what light do they need to behold what you do?

— *Epictetus*

Christmas soon followed my November diagnosis. It was not to be a normal Christmas by any means, and Cindy eventually wrote a story about it that was circulated throughout the Internet. We were amazed at how many people read the story and emailed us back with support. The story was eventually picked up and retold as part of Brad and Sherry Steiger's *Christmas Miracles: Inspirational stories of True Holiday Magic* published in 2001. Later, in December 2005, Sherry Steiger shared and discussed the story at length on the syndicated radio show Coast to Coast with George Noory. Because the story is now so well known, we decided to let you read it the way it was originally told, in Cindy's words, back in 2000.

Christmas 2000

Let me tell you about the snowy Christmas Day that we were blessed by a healing visit from a true Christmas Angel and the miracle that she blessed us with. We now know that miracles do happen, and that if you are open to receiving, they can come at any time! I'll give you a little background so you can understand the blessing we received that day! David was recently diagnosed with Stage 4 lung and bone cancer. Radiation 5 days a week and once-a-week chemotherapy treatments had been leaving him quite drained.

Because both radiation and chemotherapy treatments deplete the white blood cells that help fight infection, if David got sick he wouldn't have the ability to fight off the infection. It would be silly to die of pneumonia while healing his cancer! We all know that not only is Christmas a time of sharing love, it is also known as a time of sharing germs (especially from the wonderfully loving children in the family). Now, don't get me wrong, I love the little ones, yet we decided that Christmas with the family was not in our best interests this year. I knew that I probably could have gone myself, but I really didn't want to leave David alone for Christmas Day. As the 6-hour round trip and a few hours visit would take most the day, I made plans to go the day after Christmas. Most of the family would still be there, but all the extra visitors would not. This was the first Christmas in my 39 years that I had missed!

Now family guilt, self-inflicted or not, is one of the worst types. I called a number of times through the day and with all the *"We miss you!"* and *"We are running behind schedule, you always keep us on track!"* the guilt kept piling on! About 5 pm Christmas night, the phone rang. I get a lot of clients calling for appointments, so on days I am not working I usually screen my calls. For some unknown reason, this time I just automatically picked up the phone.

"Hi Cindy," said an unidentified voice. As she kept talking I recognized the English accent as Kate, a very sweet massage therapist who specializes in Thai massage. "Have you ever heard of Padre Pio?" she asked. I told her that I had visited Padre Pio's Monastery when I made a trip to Italy. I knew that Padre Pio was born in the late 1800s and was one of the few twentieth-century people to have received the stigmata, the wounds that Christ had experienced on the cross. He lived until the 1960s. Padre Pio was known for his compassion and healing works. He also was known to bi-locate (be in two places at once). It is documented that during the Second World War the air force was going to accidentally bomb an area that was occupied by Allies. The fighter pilots reported a monk appearing in the air, in front of the plane, motioning to them to go back. They were so scared and shaken that they did go back and the disaster was averted! Kate then asked me if I had heard about the healing miracles that happened around a glove of Padre Pio's. This I was unaware of. Kate offered to put another woman on the phone to tell me about it.

The Glove

The woman had a very sweet and calming voice. It turned out she was Nancy Duffy, a local television personality known for her beauty, inside and out. She started to tell me about Padre Pio's glove. It seemed that when the priest who was a custodian for Padre Pio in Italy returned to his parish in Brooklyn, New York, he was given two of the gloves that Padre Pio had worn to keep the blood from the stigmata wounds from dripping on the floor. These gloves were considered a sacred object and were known to have healing properties. There were multiple stories of how the glove had healed the parishioners of this Brooklyn church. One thing that helps support this claim is the uncanny and beautiful rose scent that emanates from the glove. It grows stronger and weaker, yet is always present.

Nancy continued, telling me that the Brooklyn priest kept one glove for himself and gave one to his sister. The sister felt that it really should be available for all to benefit from. She figured that the parking lot attendant knew everyone from the parish, so he would be the best guardian for the glove. The glove shares a box with a piece of sheet that came from Padre Pio's bed, a book in which people write to Padre Pio, and one of those famous double-image pictures of Padre Pio that changes as you tilt the picture from side to side! The parking attendant's little booth used to be a shrine to Frank Sinatra, but now Frank shares his glory with Padre Pio! The attendant gives the box, full of healing goodies, to whoever needs it. Nancy's son, who had written an article on the glove, had gotten on the waiting list and so now, on Christmas, she'd had the glove for two whole days! Kate had told Nancy about David's cancer, so Nancy was calling to see if David would like to touch the miraculous glove.

Well, David was tired from a visit earlier in the day and when I mentioned that, Nancy kindly offered to come to us. Now, for those of you that don't know where we live, the locals know it as Windy Hill! Our place used to be a cross-country ski resort on top of a high hill that is often buffeted with lake-effect snow. We were currently getting hit with a very big snowstorm. The landlord was out of town for the holiday so the drive to our house hadn't been plowed. Nancy still was willing to make the trip! We gave her directions and, an hour and a half later via cell phone, we guided her into our hard-to-find driveway amid the two-foot (60cm) snowdrifts!

Nancy arrived covered with snow and bearing a canvas tote. We sat in our living room where she pulled out a wooden box with a little picture of Padre Pio on the top. She gently opened it and took out the picture, a little book, and then carefully brought out the sacred glove. At first I was surprised. It was a little tiny brown glove with no fingers in it. It looked like a glove you would see on a homeless person. The funny thing to me was that it was so simple. You would think it would be ornate, or at least a little bigger! Padre Pio was a large man. I remembered seeing his slippers when I visited his monk cell in Italy. They were so big!

The little brown glove had a simple metal cross gently sewn onto the top side. Later, when I turned it over, I saw that someone had sewn a tiny piece of cloth with a little" x" in the place that must have been where the hand wound from the stigmata was. The amazing thing to us was the aroma that came from the glove. Anyone who's smelled this rose scent could tell you that it's like no other rose aroma you have ever inhaled. You couldn't re-create it, even with the best of oils or perfume. The piece of sheet from Padre Pio's bed also had that intense aroma. The sheet was in a little plastic bag, but the glove was naked except for the cross sewn to it.

David put the glove in between his hands and you could just feel the calm that came over him. This is how he explained it to me:

"At first, I sensed a type of love similar to what I feel when I reach out with my heart and touch the light I experienced in my near death. As I touched the glove I was purposely feeling with my heart and not my mind. I could sense my heart opening up and feeling that light and love. I could feel both spiritual love and human emotion and there were vast amounts of unconditional love. It is like going back into the Light a little bit, not all the way. I have been having trouble keeping my heart open and work-ing with my light and love because of the physical fatigue and drug-induced emotions associated with the treatment. The drugs have been blocking my ability to hear Spirit. As I stroked the glove, it felt like some of the barriers were just melting away and the light in my heart was able to open and shine as bright as ever. Well! I could just say that my spirit was singing. Spirit gets in this joyous frame of—not mind, but…Spirit. When Spirit is joyous, it feels like a song in my heart, interacting with my human emo-tions. It brings tears to the corners of my eyes. It gets me a little choked up. You can feel it emanate throughout your whole body. It isn't just your heart expanding; it physically expands throughout your entire body."

As our new friend Nancy told David the glove's story and how she ended up with it, he sat and stroked the sacred glove as it lay in his right hand. Later he told me he could actually feel the glove, which is its own little miracle, as he has permanent nerve damage in that hand and hasn't felt any sensation in it since his spine collapsed!

Nancy told us how Padre Pio was able to bring his compassion and insight into the confessional and would help people know what it is that they really want to release. Later David told me, *"The funny thing was that it was almost like I was giving a little confession, when I was talking to Nancy about my near-death experi-ence, cancer and what life has been like. When she told us about Padre Pio giving confessions from his heart, I felt compelled to talk about the NDE and give a confession of it. I didn't realize that till afterward."*

David handed me the glove and I could immediately feel the energy coming from the center of it. I felt calm and at peace. I knew this was real. I handed the glove back to David and then took the piece of sheet in the little bag. Again, I was taken aback by the indescribably intense rose scent growing in the room as she and David talked about everything, from how his near-death experience is helping him deal with a terminal disease to the wonderful experiences she has had while the glove has been with her. She said she felt like a Christmas Angel. We told her that she was definitely our Christmas Angel! The rose scent kept growing stronger and stronger and was starting to fill the room. It was accompanied by a pervading sense of peace and love.

At one point Nancy stopped the conversation and said, "I have had this glove for two days and the rose scent has grown stronger and weaker depending on who was holding it, but I have never smelled it this strong!" She was amazed. The scent had filled the whole room by now—and so had the sense of peace and love!

Together we shared stories, feelings, hot tea, and fresh baked ginger bread cookies as if we were old friends. An hour and half later, our Christmas Angel was calling the next person she was going to share the glove with to let them know she was on her way! We wondered if she had been able to spend any holiday time with her family, though with the number of people she had visited, we doubted she had.

After she was well on her way to share the healing glove with the next blessed person, we could still smell the rose scent and feel the peace and love.

That night, when we went to bed, David told me that he could still smell the roses. I told him that I could not smell them, yet when I reached over to touch his hand, the minute I made contact, I could smell the roses too! I slept through the rest of the miracle, but here is how David explained it to me the next day:

"I could smell the roses as we went to bed. It helped me go into a really nice calm, peaceful sleep. It assisted my body to relax and drift off to sleep, which was a lot closer to normal than in a very long time. I don't just drop off to sleep that easily lately. I used to be able to go to sleep as soon as my head hit the pillow, now I have to wait until the pain and spasms subside. That night I went right to sleep and it reminded me of when we used to do pipe ceremony. It was very comforting. The smell of the roses and the memory of the glove comforted me. I was able to get the first restful sleep in months.

At two o'clock I awoke and the smell of roses was everywhere. I started to cry quietly so as not to wake you. I could feel my heart fully open and my light and spirit shining as bright as in my near death. So, I got up, meditated, and just enjoyed taking that energy in. It has helped me since to keep my heart more open when I am feeling the physical and drug-related difficulties that are associated with the cancer therapies I am now on. That is also how the glove is continuing to help me now."

As we talked about our Christmas miracle, we realized that part of the miracle was that I was even home to get the call! If I had followed my guilt (David was feeling a little guilty, too) and had gone to my family on Christmas Day after all, we would have missed the phone call and our Christmas miracle altogether! As it was, I went down the day after Christmas and had a wonderful visit with my family and two friends! The kids were downstairs for most of the visit (thank you, Kay and Gigi) and David got to have some quiet time alone to take in all the love, peace, and light offered from the previous day!

We also talked about our Christmas miracle acting as a sign, to let us know we are right where we need to be. We feel that David's cancer has brought about a situation that is allowing us to come back to our spiritual center. We are allowing ourselves to enjoy every day, communicate our love more frequently and sincerely, and to accept all the gifts from not only God but also all of our friends and family. We are adjusting our priorities and are hopeful that David will receive the gift of full remission. We recognize our Christmas miracle as a sign that miracles do happen and that people like our Christmas Angel are around to bring miracles to us and everyone else on a daily basis. We are reminded that Angels don't always have wings — sometimes they appear in a snow-covered coat and scarf!

The Miracle Continues

A week or so after our magical visit, we had an opportunity to chat with our Christmas Angel! As we spoke on the phone, her voice brought back all the warm and loving feelings of our evening together. She told us how being the courier of the glove has touched her deeply. I was mesmerized as she recounted conversations with some of the people she had visited. Two had miracle stories of their own!

The first miracle she relayed was of a woman who had been suffering from double vision. After she held the glove, her vision was miraculously repaired. She was no longer seeing double! The woman was so overjoyed that she was almost afraid to tell anyone, in case the miracle went away. Well, she told and her vision was still clear! The second miracle story was a double of its own kind. Our Christmas Angel made a visit to a woman who has a friend with a tumor, who was unable to travel, so Nancy and the woman called her on the phone. Together, while one held the glove, they prayed for healing. When the woman with the tumor went to the doctor, the tumor was gone. The doctor had no way of explaining this miraculous disappearance, but the woman knew. Padre Pio's glove had healed again!

As I recall our magical visit from our Christmas Angel and the miracles she relayed to us, a loving and almost mystical calm comes over me. We have had many letters from people who have read our story and were very touched. The flow of miracles seems to continue even though the glove has since disappeared!

I was telling one of my clients about our Christmas miracle. She was instantly reminded that about three months ago someone had given her a medallion of Padre Pio's for her daughter, who has neurological impairments. She said that she had been carrying this medallion around in her purse and never thought to have her daughter hold it like David held the glove. She asked me to hold on while she went and got the medallion. She hadn't taken it out of the box. I felt as if I was getting to experience the blessing of last Christmas all over again! She came back to the phone and sounded as though she was in shock. She had opened the case and what she smelled sent shivers up and down both our spines. Roses. She smelled roses. Her daughter was being fussy in the background and my client decided to put the medallion in her daughter's hand. Instantly the girl calmed down and started her version of talking.

My client and I sat, in two different states, in silence. I felt as if our Christmas miracle was being passed on. My client said to me that she had realized, as she was getting the medallion out of her purse, that the medallion must go back to the woman who originally gave it to her. It turns out that the woman had been diagnosed with cancer. My client realized that the medallion didn't need to be hoarded; it needed to be shared. She was going to return the medallion in the next few days. The miracle would be passed on. My client was truly demonstrating the true spirit of Christmas.

Months later we learned a bigger miracle was on the horizon, revealed when the doctor looked at David's CAT scan.

—*Cindy Griffith-Bennett*

Chapter Eleven

❀ REMISSION ❀

In the joy of your heart may you feel the living joy that sang one spring morning, sending its glad voice across a hundred years.
— *Rabindranath Tagore*

When I think back on Christmas 2000 and how Padre Pio's glove unexpectedly came into our home, I know it came as a gift from the Universe. What I mean is that sometimes when we are exactly where we need to be on our life's path, we are given gifts of confirmation and affirmation. When I saw in my near-death life review that I was going to have to deal with cancer in this life, I had no idea how bad the cancer was going to be. When the doctors told me that the cancer had metastasized, eating away part of my spine and growing quickly, the extent of the damage meant I had a long ordeal in front of me. Knowing what I had seen in my NDE, I had faith I would survive this. By Christmas time, the treatments and the pain were beginning to take their toll. Even knowing that I would survive, my mind was starting to doubt whether I could stay the course.

That doubt was present when Padre Pio's glove came into my life. When our home filled with the scent of roses, it filled me with hope. I spent part of the next day looking and sniffing through the house to see if anything rose-scented might explain the divinely glorious aroma. I wanted to make sure nothing we owned was rose-scented and could discount the experience, but after an extensive search I found nothing. The scent was such a strong influence that we even went so far as trying to purchase a candle or perfume that smelled the same. Nothing came close to the aroma that we were treated to that night. The scent was as if we lived in a garden of roses, dripping with dew. We have yet to find any scent as divine, commercially available. The experience of the glove opened my heart again and filled me with the strength and hope I needed to continue.

This was a confirmation of *"Yes, I am right where I am supposed to be."* I knew that when I needed strength, the guidance and insights would be there for me. That understanding quieted the doubts in my mind. The scent of roses may seem like a small miracle, but it played a major role in my healing, even with the long-term effects that lay ahead.

               ಎ   ೱ

I kept trying to find statistics about lung cancer patients and five-year surviv-ability studies. I knew the data was out there, and eventually I found it online. But every time I'd try to download the information, my computer would crash. I finally gave up. I believe the Universe blocked my human need to know main-stream expectations about lung and bone cancer, and that I had to keep my faith in my own survival undeterred. Today I know that the five-year surviv-ability rate is less than one percent. That means less than one percent of people are expected to survive five years with lung and bone cancer. No wonder the Universe did not want my engineer's mind to see that information as it would have planted the seeds of doubt. I needed my visualizations and prayers to be doubt-free and keep the positive intentions of healing flowing. I needed my clear vision of living beyond the cancer and a broken spine. Not knowing freed my mind from that weight.

After the holidays, Spirit began telling me there was some improvement with the tumors. We asked the doctors to perform a CAT scan so we could know more. But the scan was not scheduled. We persisted for two months, and then, once the hospital realized insurance would pay for it, they begrudgingly scheduled a scan to appease us. But when the results came back, no one read the report, because in the medical team's reality there was no way I was going to recover. Aside from that, none of our team wanted to give us more bad news. This was incredibly frustrating for Cindy, who vowed not to be deterred from getting the results. I was developing a new philosophy of going with the universal flow. This of course frus-trated Cindy even more. Remember, the health care team believed I was in denial.

Finally, about a month after the CAT scan, we saw an oncology nurse who was a brother to one of the techs that had worked for me in the dialysis program. We were able to convince him to look at the results. By hospital regulations he couldn't tell us exactly what the results said, but he confided that the news was good. He promised he would encourage my doctor to read the results.

The doctor was shocked. The report indicated that the mass had shrunk con-siderably. Of course this led to the decision that I needed more tests. We didn't see the irony at first because we were so excited to be moving forward. A PET scan was next. In this test they infuse radioisotopes into your body that light up all of the active cancer cells. They scanned me from head to toe, and this time there was no delay to read the tests.

The PET scan indicated no active cancer cells in my body. The doctors blinked, not yet ready to become believers, and decided to give me a few more chemo treatments just in case. They even considered giving me one more complete set of chemo treatments. They felt that was the prudent thing to do because without chemo you don't get to this point, they claimed, it just doesn't happen. That is when I put my foot down and decided I'd had enough chemo.

I've learned doctors never tell Stage 4 survivors *"you're in remission"*; and they never used those words with me. What they like to say is *"you're doing very well…"* But here I am today, in remission. There, I said it, even if they will not. To this day they expect my cancer to explode and take off again. Again, that is their reality, which is based on normal outcomes. Cindy and I did not subscribe to that belief and continue to disregard the normal outcomes.

Accepting that I had to go through the treatments became part of my voyage of purpose. This stage of my life proved a major confirmation of the truth and reality of my NDE. To see and overcome such huge obstacles was incredibly humbling. I had some long talks with Spirit and made an agreement that I would continue to follow a path of communication and share what I had learned in my experiences with near-death survivors and cancer patients. Just like after I almost drowned I had an overwhelming desire to give something back, yet now the call to be of service was amplified tenfold.

Before my diagnosis of cancer, I had started a website about my NDE. I thought that was a way to reach a lot of people without having to personally be in front of them. But Spirit was directing me to speak publicly, so that others could not only hear the words but also experience my energy and light. Spirit threw in some synchronistic friends to tell me the same thing. Once I connected the messages with my purpose and understood them, I had to do more than listen passively—I had to agree that I would make communication my top priority and act on it whenever I was asked.

I thought I was being smart by making this agreement with Spirit. In my mind I didn't think anyone would actually ask because I had no plans to actively promote myself. Boy, was I wrong. But first I still had a broken spine to deal with.

I Just Want to Swim

The hero is he who lives in the inward sphere of things, in the True, Divine, Eternal, which exists always… His life is a piece of the everlasting heart of nature itself.

— Thomas Carlyle

My stamina had been virtually destroyed by my cancer treatments. On my own I was making no progress building up any endurance and I was frustrated about it. Close to six months after the last chemo treatment, I decided to go to the gym and try to regain some of my strength. Among the forms I had to sign one asked if I had any back troubles. Being that I am an honest person and truth is a main aspect of life for me, I had to say yes. The truth required an approval from my doctor before I could become a member. I didn't have to wait long because I was seeing my doctor every few weeks. So at my next checkup I said, *"Hey Doc, how about signing this paper so I can go swimming at the gym?"* My doctor replied *"Gym? Didn't you have a back problem even before the cancer? We'd better send you to an orthopedic doctor before I sign anything."*

So off I went to get x-rays at the orthopedist's office. The orthopedist took one look at the results and referred me to an orthopedic surgeon who informed me, *"One wrong sneeze and you'll be a quadriplegic."* Hey, besides that being kind of scary, there was no way I was getting my permission slip signed now! I felt as if I were in a Seinfeld episode being told *"No Gym For You!"* In fact, I was getting submitted to the hospital for a pre-surgery workup instead.

The doctors had discovered that not only did I have a collapsed spine from the loss of bone, but in my years of commercial diving I had apparently developed degenerative bone disease in my neck. My spine was so bad that it was very close to pinching off the spinal cord. The up side of all this was that they could fix both conditions with two surgeries. The first was a multiple cervical spine fusion. The second was more intense. They inserted titanium constructs with screws and did bone grafts to stabilize the thoracic spine where the cancer had eaten away the T2 and T3 vertebrae. Because of complications from the radiation therapy, I ended up having a third surgery, all within five weeks.

This left me in a wheelchair, with a brace from my chin down to my belt. I sure wouldn't go swimming in that contraption—I'd sink to the bottom! (Come to think of it, sounds a bit like how all this started.) I lived and slept with that brace for a long time. Fortunately, I had my communication with Spirit and the Hour of the Wolf to keep me occupied.

I immediately learned I did not care to be in a wheelchair. But Cindy would urge me to get out of the house and go places like the mall and the zoo. The zoo, a long loop around all the animal exhibits, was a challenge. Of course, it's all handi-capped accessible, but the paths go over hill and dale and over wooden bridges. I tried to propel my chair along, battling the fatigue that was always close at hand. Cindy had all she could do to keep me from rocketing down the gentle slopes and used every bit of her strength to help get me up the hills. Do you realize that when you are in a wheelchair you're the same height as a small child? This became very apparent to me as excited children ran by me to the next exhibit to get the best view. None of the kids wanted to be behind me, so more than once they would suddenly cut me off and most of the time they would misjudge the footrests on my chair, sending a sudden jolt through to my immobilized body. That outing made me gun-shy of little kids.

Months later after the brace came off, I had to learn how to stand up and walk again. I had physical therapy at home until I was well enough to get into town. I finally was getting some exercise, but this wasn't how I planned it. By the way, I think all physical therapists have a little sadist in them (oh but wait—that would be a judgment, so throw it away!). I bless my therapist for pushing the envelope of my endurance. Without therapists and Cindy I would not have gotten very far.

ॐ   ॐ

We all have those times in our lives when everything is turned upside down. My NDE, surviving cancer, and being confined in a wheelchair were my times. When you're in one of those times, it is like the world has stopped for you, it's a time you need to be extra gentle with yourself. You may be watching the world go by in some sense, but you are still connected to a higher level. When something in your whole being has changed you can see more clearly and get more from each experience. As I was learning to live life with new physical limitations, for example, I found ways to expand my mindfulness practice.

In earlier chapters I spoke about mindfulness as being aware and in the present moment, because in the next moment your present time will only be a memory, a piece of the past. During a spiritually transformative event, you can see the influence of your present moment before it has passed because of your connection to the Oneness. You ask yourself, what can I learn from this? How can I use this in my everyday mindfulness? I was shown how I could use gentle and non-judgmental labels for those whispers of our mind that we know as thinking.

Teaching the mind gentle labels and letting go can be an approach that is much different from affirmations and mantras. In those approaches we train our minds to think a certain way. This way we learn to release negative thoughts. When in the present moment, we often hear our thoughts as colossal, passion-filled events, yet we can let them go, as a dream that does not need to be realized.

If we label our mind's performance as "Thoughts," then we can see the emotion and aggression attached to them simply as "Reactions." This sounds easier than it is in practice. When I am having an emotion-driven thought, my mindfulness can easily be left in the dust. If you start attaching a label to your thoughts, however, you will achieve a level of mindfulness. By labeling, you can turn your heated emotions and aggressions—Reactions—into compassion, thereby under-standing others on their paths. This is the way to an awakened heart. It helps to remember that everyone's path is personal, between him or her and their Creator, and unknowable to the rest of us.

Here is an everyday example: I'm in a store and I overhear someone aggressive-ly speaking to the person beside him or her. My mind immediately tells me, *"This antagonist is out of place and should be dealt with."* I can feel the emotional heat of anger welling up inside. That emotion and anger now inside me could carry on for minutes or hours depending how long I hold on to it. For all I know, this drama in the store might be a turning point for this person's path and a necessary action. If I hear the critical thoughts as my "judgmental mind," then I can imme-diately label it as a Thought. Then I'm able to maintain my center. The anger and emotion Reaction does not need to be acted upon, or fulfilled. Maybe, if it's ap-propriate, I can take action, but sometimes not reacting is the appropriate move.

I've learned to use the labeling gently, as a way to acknowledge the dramas in my life as stories my mind has made up to distract me. When something starts brewing in my mind, I can let it go sooner if I label it. With practice and dis-cipline the letting go happens quicker each time. The more I label the negative thoughts of the mind, the more centered I am in my life.

No matter what you are cooking up that could lead to the wrong action, let it go. Most of the time the negative stories of the mind are incorrect anyway. This works both ways, for positive as well as negative thoughts. If something wonderful hap-pens, then share it and let it go as well before you start grasping it. When I started to disregard the dramas in life, I found the dramas no longer sought me out. More and more I stopped acting like the Energizer Bunny running around banging the drum. I guess you might say I'm coming closer to a fully awakened heart.

Stand Up

Life is a voyage. The winds of life come strong
From every point; yet each will speed thy course along,
If thou with steady hand when tempests blow
Canst keep thy course aright and never once let go.
— Theodore Chickering Williams

After a considerable amount of time in physical therapy, I got a walker to replace my wheelchair, then a cane and eventually freedom. I could walk again on my own two numb feet. Stabilizing the spine did not repair the neuropathy. Mindful-ness became even more essential in my life as I again became mobile. Without being able to feel my feet and hands I needed to be focused on each step and how to hold things in my hands. If I become tired or lose focus I either fall down or drop things. It is amazing what we can accomplish once we apply our *intention* and focus. I also used my mindfulness practice to assist me in managing my pain. After the surgeries healed, the pain was lessoned a great deal, but I still had an on-going level of chronic pain. To top it off, everywhere the surgeries were performed I developed arthritis.

Focusing on each step I took showed me the way to manage my pain without medication. To walk without watching my feet, I use the pressure on my heels and ankles to know what my feet are doing. That takes constant focus, and mindfulness is made to order for that. By concentrating so much on my walking, I realized the pain had been set aside. Spirit showed me how to set my intention every morning when I rise from bed: embrace the pain and then set it aside. I know the pain is there, and it reminds me to not do silly things that might hurt me further. However, if I *speak* about the pain it brings it back into my mental awareness and I suffer. Then I have to reapply the intention of setting the pain aside. The only time this is difficult is when I'm experiencing extreme fatigue.

I was satisfied with the tools Spirit and I had developed and started forging a new life. After a few years I began to believe that I'd done a great job in healing and that this was as far as my healing could go. But I was to have another wonderful yet humbling experience. My ego has a way of slipping into my life and creating obstacles I didn't even know were there. Throughout most of my adult life I have suffered from Restless Leg Syndrome. It is a family trait, my mother suffered with it most of her life and took all sorts of medications for it. The cancer fired up my RLS, so I was taking low doses of amitriptyline, which only work some of the time. One day Dave Seaward, a friend of ours, told us about another friend, Debra Crossman, who had RLS and how she went to Rev. Jane Suprynowicz, who used the Yuen Method of energy healing. This unique healing technique (often called a correction) can eliminate or lessen pain in minutes. I had known Rev. Jane since my second near-death experience. We saw each other a couple times a years at holistic gatherings, where I frequently would give a talk about NDEs.

I made an appointment with Jane, and we discussed all my health issues, not just my jumpy legs. Then she stepped behind me, outside my field of vision. As she started her healing method, I focused on releasing my intention to set my pain aside so my energy did not interfere with the healing process. As soon as I let go, I sensed warmth generating at the base of my spine. Slowly, this warm energy started moving down the back of my legs. I sat there, immobile in my seat, not wanting to move for fear it would break the flow of healing energy. The wave of warmth moved all the way down my legs and into my feet. Then wave after wave of energy kept coursing down the back of my legs. I was merely an observer of this energy transference. Then I suddenly noticed I could feel my socks. I hadn't felt the socks on my feet for years. I kept my body absolutely still but I couldn't stop wiggling my toes. I had the biggest grin on my face, and it was all I could do to keep from cheering in excitement. A few moments later Rev. Jane came around from behind me and softly asked, *"How was that?"* I shouted out, *"I can feel my toes —it's amazing!"* She quietly said, *"Yes, I know."* I jumped up and gave her a giant hug. That night I decided to not take any medication for my Restless Leg Syndrome, and I experienced the best night's sleep I could remember. Not only that night, but every night since. Once in a great while I'll feel a slight twinge in my legs but nothing bothersome.

Once I settled down I had to face the fact that Rev. Jane's energetic healing was beyond what I had been able to accomplish on my own. I realized I had forgotten to ask others for help. We all have friends who want to help us in times of need. I had asked my friends to pray and send me light when I was originally diagnosed, but now that the cancer was gone and the surgeries were over, when people asked how I was feeling, my habitual reply was always a short and polite, "Fine." My ego had blinded me to the interconnection we all share, and I was not allowing my friends to continue to share their love and light. That was incredibly selfish of me and I had to acknowledge my mistake. One of our greatest gifts from the One-ness is our interconnection and ability to share our gifts of love with each other.

This thought overwhelmed my ego, dispelling it while humbling and opening my awareness to something I had forgotten. The lesson was to stay open to all opportunities. I no longer discount any experience as minor and always accept help with gratitude.

Scar, the Humpback Whale

Where one realizes the indivisible unity of life, sees nothing else, hears nothing else, knows nothing else, that is the Infinite. Where one sees separateness, hears separateness, knows separateness, that is finite. The Infinite is beyond death, but the finite cannot escape death.

— *Chandogya Upanishad*

The Scar story happened before my near-death experience, but it is a good ex-ample of why we should not take any experience for granted, or treat it as minor. Now, with the help of Spirit, I see this event much differently. I now understand it as a rewarding experience and want to share it.

Once upon a time, back when I was the chief engineer of a research vessel, we were working with a small tethered submarine off the New England Coast. As we arrived at the work site we noticed the humpback whales were migrating along the coast. One whale in particular became well known to us, and we nicknamed her Scar. She apparently had come close to the sightseeing boats one too many times: her body was covered with propeller scars. We figured that Scar was either very friendly or incredibly stupid, and a nuisance to shipping.

We were working on the ocean floor with our remote-operated submarine (ROV). Part of the job required us to launch the submarine every day so we could survey the ocean floor. To launch, we lowered the ROV and its cage into the water. After the cage was submerged the small submarine would undock from the cage. Then remote operators would fly/swim the submarine to the sea floor. My job as chief engineer was to ensure that the submarine was in proper working order. After the submarine was in the water I would normally attend to other ship duties. But Scar made this particular survey job different.

When the submarine started to work its way down, Scar would swim under it and begin bringing it back to the surface. This of course drove the remote operators crazy. Scar thought the small sub was a baby whale and she was trying to bring it to the surface so the baby could breathe. She didn't want the ROV to swim too deep, and she was trying to help it. There was no way they could keep Scar from doing this, and it was wasting valuable time and money.

The scientists and the operators could not think of any way to stop Scar. Then someone had a bright idea that maybe a diver could distract Scar long enough so that we could get the sub to the bottom. The few times before that we got it to the bottom Scar would leave it alone, so it seemed like a logical plan.

I was the lucky guy chosen to dive and distract Scar. Before we launched the submarine each day, I got into our Zodiac and fooled around to attract Scar. When Scar came, she would roll on her side so she could look at me with her huge eye. When Scar looked at me that way, I felt as if she were looking into my soul. It was a strange yet wonderful feeling. I would then get out of the boat and swim with her until the ROV was on the bottom.

Although we all thought there must be something wrong with Scar to hang around boats, no one wished her any harm. After a few days of interaction with me in the Zodiac she no longer came by to visit. The call of migration and her natural rhythms probably pulled her away. But we all joked about her dumb stunts for months.

Now, many years after my near-death experience, Spirit brought up Scar. Spirit helped me see how this life experience was meant to demonstrate unconditional love, the infinite power of the universe, and the beauty of nature. Scar was not crazy, and there was nothing wrong with her. As I recall her eye looking at me, I can feel her unconditional love. The strength of love overcame her fear of us. One of Scar's roles in the universe was to show everyone how beautiful a humpback whale is. She would roll on her side and take a look at us. She was willing to undergo the pain of being run over just so she could look at us and communicate love through her stunning eyes.

I see you Scar. She showed us what beauty and love is. I wish I had understood this when it was happening so I could have helped my shipmates understand that Scar wasn't crazy.

Everything we do in life is meant to either give love or receive love. Whether it is in our work or play we are always trying to give love or receive love. Every action a human makes or tries to make is predicated on wanting to be loved. The societies humankind has built are built on human emotions. As messed up as that might seem in reality, it gives us all the ability to live the life we choose to live. Every act we perform is a call for love. Even the emotions that are negative—greed, hatred and hostility—are ends to a means for love. We do this to make ourselves into what we think will make us be loved or give love. Even hobbies like gardening or cooking, or the intense effort you put into work, are meant to make you into the person who will receive love or be able to give love. In the universe love is everything and everything is love, so when you can love unconditionally you will be a different person, and you will have made a giant step forward for all humanity.

Unconditional love is larger than we are. We have trouble understanding it. Unconditional love is endless and unifies everyone and everything in this universe. It's hard for us to constantly feel unconditional love as humans; conditionally using love is easier, simpler. We keep adding a step to our love—wanting something in return or something else—and making it complicated. Maybe that's why so many think of love as troublesome. It would be much simpler to love unconditionally. If we expected nothing in return for our love, it would be a truer more powerful love, and more like the infinite power of the universe.

Chapter Twelve

❀ TIME TO COMMUNICATE ❀

Joy exists to show that the bonds of law can only be explained by love; they are like body and soul. Joy is the realization of the truth of oneness, the oneness of our soul with the world and of the world-soul with the supreme lover.

— *Rabindranath Tagore*

Through my near-death experience and dealing with health issues I learned that I can use my difficulties and problems to awaken my heart and make it stronger, so that I do not need to shield or protect it. By opening my heart, I widen my circle of compassion. If I can develop unconditional compassion for myself first, that leads naturally toward unconditional compassion for others.

Compassion for others comes from the realization of our kinship with all beings. We may feel we are the lowest wretches on this earth or at the lowest point in our lives, but we can bring everything, all of that, to awaken our hearts and be aware. We need to stop criticizing and blaming our lives, while not ignoring or running away from life.

I try to examine the moment I'm in, and as I observe this moment, an *exceptional* moment, I discover an enormous and powerful space in which to live my life. A space opens where everything exists and from which all possibilities *have* the capacity to flow outward. The idea that we are isolated beings is incorrect, a huge misunderstanding—we all have an interconnectedness to everything.

Opening your heart and being present in every moment is an enormous goal to set for yourself. Start with an open mind and look closely at the present moment. You'll begin to see the craving, suffering, aggression, and denial in others and ourselves. This is not easy, but you must accept yourself as you are before you can move forward to make yourself the best you can be. If you can accept who you are then you are ready to begin being more aware.

The Buddhist calls this awareness *bodhichitta*, or awakened heart. Each and every one of us has what we need right now to awaken our hearts. We just need to acknowledge it. We spend a huge amount of time searching for our heart connection somewhere else. We look in books, go to retreats, look to lovers or teachers for the answers. When anyone talks about enlightenment or awakening the *bodhichitta*, all they are trying to say is, *"We know it is here within us."* Eventually we come to realize that our connection has been here all along. What we are really looking for is a way to make a connection to our light, our true being.

A Chinese proverb says, *"There are many paths to the top of the mountain, but the view is always the same."* That is, although different solutions to a problem or question may exist, the answer is always the same! Finding your connection to your true being is different for everyone—there is not just one-way. That is why so many perceive it as a difficult voyage. Finding your awakened heart is a journey in itself, building upon your spiritual development. I have yet to find someone on the path that hasn't had a spiritual revelation or two while making his or her connection. A central theme for many on the path is going inward and finding a sacred silence within through meditation or contemplation. I can always tell when my light connection is there because I have a feeling of expansion within myself. Many times I feel it in my heart. We all have the ability of *bodhichitta* within us. Awareness is an innate skill, we are born with it, and we only have to find the doorway to it once. Then we can open it at will whenever the need arises.

So as I said earlier we can use our difficulties and problems to awaken our heart and make it stronger. When do we look for guidance? Is it when we are suffering the most? We need to change our thoughts about suffering and learn to turn it around so we can then embrace it. Running away from suffering only prolongs it. I learned we should face the difficulty, look at it deeply and clearly so we can rise above the problem. As we come to new understandings of our troubles they no longer give the same pain because that mental gap we spoke of before, where everything exists and all possibilities flow, has opened in our consciousness and loving clarity comes pouring in. We must be willing to not only endure it but also take our new understandings and let them stimulate and awaken our heart, let them soften instead of hardening us against suffering. At this point we can learn to embrace it. We will start to feel unconditional compassion for ourself and, eventually, for others.

Yes, we can use our difficulties and problems to awaken the heart and make it stronger.

Letting Go

Where there is a way or a path, it's someone else's way.... I have a theory that if you are on your own path things are going to come to you. Since it's your own path, and no one has ever been on it before, there's no precedent, so everything that happens is a surprise and is timely.

— Joseph Campbell

When we experience something pleasant, we want to hold on to it and not let go. We are afraid if we let go we might lose that pleasantness. Some of the most miserable folks are those who have a lot of material things and, they fear, a lot to lose. If you are enjoying what you are experiencing in life, then be generous and think of others. Share the wealth and joy—a big piece of the spiritual path is giving back what you have learned and sharing it. The harder we grasp something the more it crumbles and slips through our fingers.

A friend and I were talking about suffering; I was listening to him speak about winning a long fight. He had recently gone through a legal battle. I asked if he had taken on a lot of armament for the battle. Yes, he had, he'd gathered a huge defense. I then asked what he had done with the defenses now that the battle was won. He said he was keeping the defenses, to keep his guard up. I told him my idea that how we live is how we take care of our heart. Often, once we are victorious, we keep guarding our heart, shielding and armoring it. So have we really won the war? I could sense my friend's energy and see the wounds of the battle were still with him, he was not allowing them to heal. The heart can be so protected that nothing can touch it. I told him that one thing I've learned is that when you let go of your shields your suffering will soon unravel. Don't be afraid of something touching your soft spot. You need to let go of all those defenses you have gathered or you will have difficulty achieving an awakened heart. True wealth is allowing everything to touch your heart.

Those who possess the power of an awakened heart and trust their truth, grasp that control lightly. They understand that by clutching or holding on to an idea of power, one becomes possessed by it. Wiser individuals do not need to defend who or what they are because they are confident of their truth within. Once we understand we no longer need to fight against jealousy or insult, we can self-examine and choose to maintain the dignity of our inner peace.

Another way of denying the heart is to accept programming—by advertising, movies, fashion etc. — that we need to be someone else. We are taught to look like something we are not, or we need to project a false sense of self. It's the same old trap and we are not living within our truth. We may project that we are something wonderful but inside we are judging ourselves as something less. We need to accept who we are and support our truth. It will be painful at first but we must embrace the pain, so that it might touch our heart and get through. Touching the heart is the point, after all, isn't it?

Releasing Fear

*Be careful what you water your dreams with. Water them with worry
and fear and you will produce weeds that choke the life from your dream.
Water them with optimism and solutions and you will cultivate success.
Always be on the lookout for ways to turn a problem into an opportunity
for success. Always be on the lookout for ways to nurture your dream.*

— *Lao Tzu*

After cancer and three back surgeries, I had to accept that there was no way I was
going back to work. I have neuropathy in my hands and feet, a limited range of
motion in my neck and back, plus new titanium constructs for a spine. Operating
on one lung leaves me short of stamina and the medical community considers
me permanently disabled. However, I am not a person to sit around the house
and do nothing. I had made a commitment to Spirit to communicate with others
and I intended to keep my promise. Given my physical limitations, developing a
personal website seemed to be the best way I could communicate and reach out
to other experiencers and survivors.

I'm continually asked, "What made it easier for you to speak about your near-
death experience (NDE) so openly?" Many who've had an NDE find speaking to
others difficult. There is always a nagging fear that people are going to think we're
nuts and criticize or belittle us. I'm sorry to say this fear is justified, even today.
Although the NDE is very large and life-changing for us, and we want to share
the love and message from it, many of us are apprehensive about talking about it.
Most of the time, however, if an experiencer is asked questions in an open, non-
pushy and respectful manner, he or she is more than willing to speak about their
experience. It is too bad that some people fear the unknown we have faced and
cannot benefit from our experiences.

Experiencers have glimpsed the Universal Consciousness and then faced a
radical shift in reality and perspective. After my second NDE, I lost my marriage
and some friends who could not understand who I was anymore. It is like a seed
has been planted in our souls that we cannot escape. We try to fit in but life is not
the same to us anymore. The more we integrate the NDE into our being the more
it is with us every moment. We are trapped by our own need to explain it and at
the same time unable to put the experience into words. Fear and the inability to
express ourselves so others can understand us are the two most common reasons
for not speaking about an NDE.

What changed my hesitance to speak was the realization that my fear was actually the manifestation of the fear reaction in others about the unknown. Remem-

ber, we are constantly exchanging our energy with one another and we are able to sense each other's energy fields. When I am confident and without fear, I find the response from others is much more positive. I no longer expect negative reactions, even though I realize that the NDE can challenge some beliefs. I attempt to convey my message in a non-threatening manner. I have spoken with a great number of people—at lectures, on the Internet, radio and television—and I get more genuine curiosity and questions than negativity.

When others feel your fear they will react in a negative way. That's because if we broadcast fear in our energy exchanges, the reaction we expect will be manifested. However, you cannot pretend you are not fearful—you have to believe you are not and know that the result of sharing your experience will be positive. Speaking from within your love is the best way to transform your fear, as your listeners will respond to your loving intentions. Also, don't misunderstand aggressive questions as negative—in most cases it is only healthy curiosity expressed poorly.

I have also found that the more you speak about something the better you can phrase your ideas in ways that other people understand. How do you express colors and sound that don't exist in the physical world...or the sense of timelessness, Oneness, and All-knowing? Being able to put something so powerful into words comes with time and experience—and even then your words may fall short. So move ahead with what you have. It doesn't hurt to take the time needed to integrate your NDE before speaking about it publicly. It has been over twenty-eight years since my NDE and I am still integrating—and I expect my integration to continue until its time to return to the Light.

Finding Community

We were born to unite our fellowmen, and to join in community with the human race.

— Cicero

I've always regretted that I didn't have a mentor or a group of other experiencers to share with immediately after my first NDE. I eventually found them, though it took too many years. Being with other experiencers provides the comfort and support of knowing you are not alone, without the fear of ridicule. Speaking with other experiencers helps you build your vocabulary as well, so you can describe the many new things you are feeling as you integrate and work through the experience.

Finding community with other experiencers is so important to me that I became the leader of a local IANDS (International Association for Near Death Studies) group. The IANDS organization has been researching NDEs for over thirty years, which has been a tremendous service to experiencers. If there is no IANDS group in your area, you can always find a similar group or one in another state or country on the Internet. If you are really ambitious, build your own community by starting a group. It only takes you and one other experiencer to form a group. When you put the word out, you may be surprised at how many other experiencers live and work in your area that are also looking for community.

Research is showing us that the aftereffects of NDEs also occur in those who have had near-death-like experiences, such as Spiritually Transformative Experiences (STEs). These present the exact same challenges of an NDE afterward. I include all types of transformative experiences when I speak of "experiencers."

A recent study in the Journal of Near-Death Studies by Yolaine M. Stout, Linda A. Jacquin and P.M.H. Atwater showed there are six major challenges faced by experiencers. The first challenge is processing a radical shift in reality, because most experiencers face a reality unlike anything in their lives previously. Time is needed to process that, and being with other experiencers who accept and understand makes integration more comfortable. All experiencers seek to be whole again and need help bringing the old and new realities together.

The need to share the experience is another major challenge. I used to think it was funny that all experiencers I met wanted to write a book. After I started to speak publicly about my experiences, people asked if I had a book. So now here I am, with a book of my own. NDEs are so intense and provide experiencers with such a profound sense of purpose and message of love for humanity that it cannot be contained. We want our messages heard and accepted. Choosing other experiencers or someone that understands the aftereffects, as our confidants, can be very constructive.

Unfortunately, even today with all the information out there about this subject, doctors, therapists, and religious leaders still commonly diagnose experiencers as being mentally ill. We need more groups and organizations like IANDS and ACISTE to educate and support all experiencers. ACISTE (American Center for the Integration of Spiritually Transformative Experiences) is a new nonprofit organization beginning to network trained peers, mentors, group leaders, and caregivers to help address integration challenges and offers resources to enhance an experiencer's short and long-term well-being. More research into the aftereffects will better inform the health care professionals and clergy who tend to be the first people whom experiencers reach out to.

☙ ❧

When you find another experiencer, keep in touch and be supportive. Support each other with loving acceptance and non-judgment. The other person may be on a different level of integration, so allow him or her to be where they are. Help celebrate the differences in experiences because each experience is unique. Don't feel you need to know exactly what the other experiencer is talking about. Allow the person the luxury of completing his story uninterrupted. Listening is supportive and the first principle of friendship. Every experiencer feels changed by the event, and many develop new spiritual values. These changes cause stress in relationships with family and friends. So again, be supportive.

As you begin to build your community and share your own experience, you will find both experiencers and interested seekers among those who gather together. If you have already integrated your experience, people will tend to look up to you and want you to tell them what to do or make their life decisions for them. Others may try to unconsciously give over their personal power to you. Margaret Kean taught me early on not to be a guru. His Holiness the Dalai Lama told the group we were with that we should not ask him to be our teacher. We should instead think of him as our spiritual friend. Those statements stayed with me and have been a defining principle in how I present my experiences to others.

Let us all be spiritual friends.

Once you start to explore other people's NDEs, it is important not to judge your experience by theirs. Many people have said to me, *"I don't think I had a real NDE because I didn't have a tunnel"* or *"I didn't have a life review."* Research has shown that only a small percentage of experiencers actually go through a tunnel or have a life review. A near-death experience doesn't have to have all the components to be considered one. It doesn't matter if it is an Out of Body Experience (OBE) or a Spiritual Awakening. One doesn't have to be near death or die to go through the aftereffects.

I wish I had not repressed my experience for such a long time. I feel that it postponed my integration by eleven years. Even if I had started writing sooner, it would have helped. Writing is a wonderful tool for recalling details and beginning to understand the experience. Writing about my experiences, even so many years after my NDE, required a process of examination that produced many new helpful insights.

Many good books are already out there to help experiencers understand the aftereffects of their NDE. I have included a reference list of some of these books in the appendices.

Spiritually Transformative Experience

All will surely realize God. All will be liberated. It may be that some get their meal in the morning, some at noon, and some in the evening; but none will go without food. All, without any exception, will certainly know their real Self.

— *Ramakrishna*

I define an experiencer as someone who has had a life-altering event that changes his or her life permanently. That is, it affects how the person lives day-to-day on a continuous, long-term basis. Let me share a more recent set of circumstances that illustrate a spiritually transformative experience.

About twelve years ago Spirit urged me to reconnect with my mother and stepfather. I reluctantly agreed, knowing full well that they would probably push all my buttons and present one of my greatest tests. In the relationship that slowly rekindled I was not wrong to have had trepidation. I could write another book on what I learned in that relationship, but when my stepfather Jimmy passed away suddenly, I knew Spirit was perfect in the timing of our coming back together and reconciling our differences.

It's easy to say my mom didn't give much thought to the afterlife. Marge had stepped inside a church only for marriages or funerals in her ninety-two years of life and was a self-professed atheist. She was aware of my two near-death experiences and my close call with lung and bone cancer, but she never wanted to talk about it. When I began traveling to speak about my NDEs she had no more interest beyond: "You're going away again? To talk about your cancer stuff?"

Spring 2008 was a tough time for Mom. She went through a number of infections, each leaving her a little weaker. Then one day her sister-in-law found her on the floor and she had to be rushed from assisted living to the hospital with a serious infection. From there she went to a physical rehabilitation facility. She loved the attention in physical therapy and the girls there called her "Margie." Mom would tell me. "They got me pumping iron!"— her lingo for working out with stretches, weights and using the walker. She seemed to be improving a little day by day.

Late one night I received a call that she had been sent to the hospital again with yet another infection. When I got to the hospital she looked terrible. Mom didn't recognize me, in fact she thought I was her late husband Jimmy. This second infection left her even more debilitated. She had to be fed, and I was the only one she would eat or drink for—she refused to work with the medical staff.

One morning Mom was more serious than usual and it was clear she wanted to tell me something. She started out saying that she had lived a long life and was very satisfied, then went on to tell me that she did not want to continue living with the pain and suffering of one infection after another. She kept repeating the phrase "I'm going to quit this racket." I told her I understood, and if that is what she really wanted I would support her. She was very specific that yes, this is what she wanted.

After that conversation Mom stopped eating and drinking. Within a day the doctors were trying to call Mom incompetent and were strong-arming me to let them insert a feeding tube. I kept speaking with Mom and could tell she wanted to be left alone to pass away. When the doctors realized they were not going to get their way, they immediately transferred Mom back to the rehabilitation facility.

After her reevaluation the nurse practitioner thanked me for not caving in to the pressure about the feeding tube. Mom was placed on palliative care. The last few days I stayed with Mom as much as I could. We spent time listening to soothing music and reminiscing about some of the goofy stories in her life, Like her black Pomeranian, a kinetic nut that so amused us with his crazy acrobatic behavior. To our astonishment neither of us could remember his name.

I recognized that even with me present Mom still thought of herself as dying alone. The mind's state of separateness had Mom in its grip. You can't be human without sometime feeling that you are alone and only you know what your life has been all about. In the end, however, she found how untrue that notion was in the amazing last hours of her life.

On the tenth day in the rehabilitation center Mom awoke and started reaching toward the corner of the room and talking to someone. Sitting next to her bed, I turned to look at the corner, and rather than it being in shadow it was now alight and bright. Spirit comforted me and I could feel my heart open as this presence communicated with Mom. It was only a few hours later that Mom passed into the Light and went home.

I have felt Mom's presence many times, and she's come to me in dreams twice since her passing. In the first dream, a week or two after her death, she was excited and happy and she told me that King, the black Pomeranian was with her. That short conversation let me know she was doing fine.

The second dream came months later; it was much longer and even more vivid. She was with a very young girl who was leading her around. Mom was wearing heels—she was in great health and clearly did not need assistance. I didn't understand why she was being so tolerant of this young girl. It was so unlike my mother. When I woke I knew Mom was showing me how much different she was within her true being. She demonstrated a tolerance and understanding that she rarely, if ever, did in life.

A few days after the dream I was consoling a friend who had just lost her dad. She told me of her After-Death Communication dream, in which she saw her father with all of her deceased siblings. I was rocked by the realization that the little girl with my mother was the baby Mom had lost before I was born. She was the sister I never knew. With tears of love I have to give thanks to Mom for introducing us.

The universe provides us with all these amazing experiences. If we allow it, they will shape our spiritual existence while here in this physical form. If I had not had my prior experiences, these two After-Death Communications (ADCs) would have been the catalyst to send me searching for more spiritual understanding. Mom's passing and the ADCs are excellent examples of spiritually transformative experiences. I know Mom is in a great loving place after a difficult life, and I am grateful to Spirit for urging me to reconnect with my mom, Marge.

What I've Gained

Progress consists, not in the increase of truth, but in freeing it from its wrappings. The truth is obtained like gold, not by letting it grow bigger, but by washing off from it everything that isn't gold.

— *Tolstoy*

My transformational experiences shifted the direction in the way I lived my life, they came at the perfect time, showing me the bearing in which I needed to go. Most important, I now understand that at the time of death we do not really die: we live on with a higher level of consciousness. So with this understanding, I no longer fear death. Fear of death is similar to fearing your first day at school. You have anxiety, apprehension, and fear of the unknown. But those of us who die and then return get a preview of a new school and the other students. We really like the subjects taught and the other souls we found there. We know some intense study lies ahead, but we are looking forward to it. Our time back on earth is meant for completing our pre-course requirement, which is gaining as many experiences as we can so we can bring them back to class for non-judgmental examination—when the time is right.

No longer having the fear of death offers incredible freedom, a freedom to live life unbridled and to its fullest, filled with joy and gratitude at each encounter and experience. Not fearing death also gives a sense of calm, which enables us to unwind; no longer caught up in the rat race.

Not that I do not participate and contribute in life. On the contrary, I want more than ever to live a full life. I am carrying on, through hardships and good times, overcoming and taking it all in. I try to stay as positive as I humanly can through it all. When I am able to accomplish something positive, a sense of completion follows, often accompanied by a sign that tells me the direction of a new path ahead.

If I have learned anything from my experiences it is to follow those synchronistic events in life. Even though I may not be able to see the bigger picture when it is happening, I know it will reveal itself at the right time and place. When I do connect to the greater universal consciousness, I can *physically* feel my heart opening, filling my being with Spirit's warm love and acceptance, as if I am projecting beyond my physical self. It is when I am in that place that I see my light and sometimes the light of others. It is then that Spirit speaks soft, loving encouragement to keep me moving forward and gives me the strength to take on what is next in this wondrous voyage of life.

An experience that illustrates this connection happened on a beautiful pre-dawn Sunday morning in early March. I had gone to my sugar shack to boil the sap I had collected from my maple trees the day before. This is one of my springtime rituals that gets me out of the house and back into nature, where I feel at peace. It also helps me recover my center after a long gray winter.

We live in the Finger Lake area of Central New York State (the Snow Belt to some upstate folks.) In early spring the snow cover slowly melts as the warmer air comes in from the south. This produces the most magical mornings with thick ground fog. We are also in the path of the eastern flyway for thousands of migrating birds. Just the day before Cindy and I had seen thousands of snow geese in the stubble of last year's corn crop on our neighbor's 280-acre farm.

On this particular morning, I woke and sleepily wandered down stairs, I chanced a peak out the window into the dim morning. I couldn't see past the trees just outside the window because of the fog. *"Great,"* I thought, *"I love these mystical mornings."* As I headed out to the shack I could hear the honks of some Canadian geese in flight, which only added to an already perfect morning. So, with new energy I got the fire started. Every so often a flock of geese would fly directly over head. I especially love the snow geese because they do not honk as they fly. You just hear *vizz, vizz, vizz*—the sound of their wings. When I hear that sound I love to stand in the doorway and watch as they appear out of the mist like magical beings then disappear again into the swirling vapor.

The morning energized me as I got busy with the wood for the fire. I need a hot fire in order to produce a good rolling boil in the sap pan. My sugaring rig is homemade, consisting of an old woodstove and a 12 x 20 pan that fits pretty well on top. I've rigged a cake pan above to preheat the sap and slowly feed it into the boiling pan. It's not a fancy modern evaporator, but it serves my needs of supplying the family with syrup. I have to focus to keep the fire hot enough and the sap boiling at the right level. Applying mindfulness to this process helps me center, and when I reach that mindfulness apex I can see auras of the trees and nature. I had just settled into my chair by the door when I distinctly heard Spirit say: *"Expand your awareness into the Oneness and witness the wonders of our interconnection to all."*

That phrase then kept echoing in my true being. So I stepped outside into the misty dawn, ready to touch that place within myself that connects me to the light. My awareness reached out beyond what I could see through the fog that surrounded me. I could feel the drops of condensation clinging to the branches, even though they were out of sight. I could sense the energy of the magical mist moving all around me, the waves of life force connecting the fog to me. My connection to Spirit swelled as I experienced overwhelming love and delight for nature. I heard geese flying in the distance. I expanded my awareness in that direction. I sensed the small flock of geese turn and head my way as Spirit said, *"Watch the interconnectedness of All."*

Spirit was directing the geese to fly directly overhead, and there they were, not in their normal V-formation but in a single row, flying low above me, only as high as the treetops. I felt as if I could soar and fly with them!

As they disappeared back into the mist, where I could not see them, I was carried along with them because of my expanded awareness. They began another turn in the opposite direction and headed back my way. Then once again they appeared at treetop level above my head, coming from the other direction. They completed a perfect figure eight—the infinity symbol —over my head. This was Spirit, showing me that our interconnection is infinite.

Then more flocks arrived and completed the same infinity maneuver over my sugar shack and me. All this happened in what seemed like fifteen to twenty minutes.

I realized I'd better get back to my boiling sap, as surely the fire was low. But when I stepped back inside the shack the roar of the boiling sap and the heat of the fire made it seem as if no time had passed. I savored the aroma of syrup as I returned to my boiling, but keeping my awareness focused on my connection to the All. Spirit shared more knowledge with me: *"Keep connecting and expanding your awareness. Stay in the Oneness as often as possible."* This was a message I'd heard before but this experience emphasized its importance and strengthened the meaning. *"Encourage the others who know how as well"* was more of the message.

I said my gratitude prayers and was answered with the friendly honks of a pair of geese that touched down in the field behind the sugar shack. As the morning fog cleared and the day brightened I practiced this expanded awareness. I spotted a flock of redwing blackbirds and lovingly asked them to come and sing about this beautiful day. The trees then filled with singing birds and I could feel the group mind, the connection they had to one another—again the interconnectedness. Then the geese joined in, followed by cardinals, chickadees, goldfinches, robins and a red-bellied woodpecker. I felt like a music director conducting a symphony, knowing the rise and pitch of the song… But then something broke my concentration and all the birds flew away, leaving me laughing, grateful, and loving this life.

Conversion

Remember that you ought to behave in life as you would at a banquet. As something is being passed around it comes to you; stretch out your hand, take a portion of it politely. It passes on; do not detain it. Or it has not come to you yet; do not project your desire to meet it, but wait until it comes in front of you.

— *Epictetus*

My life has been transformed through this voyage. As happened that day in the sugar shack, I am connecting to the Oneness more and more often, anticipating the unfolding of adventure with every change of tack. Recently I've received insights that allow me to view my potential paths. I liken these to *future living* insights—that is, with them I actually experience an episode in my future. Future living insights are like markers on the path, given to show I am moving in the correct direction.

Future living insights are intensely detailed, as if I were *pre*-living them. The events occur when I have undertaken a spiritual journey that aligns me with my true being. I am transported away from my present circumstances, the present me, to a potential me, to a place where I can remember my future. It is very much like remembering the past, only it is remembering in the future. I not only experience the event but the environment in which it occurs.

I believe these future living insights alert me to my soul's purpose, acting like guideposts. When a future event is actualized in my present life, it is like déjà vu on steroids. But having experienced this event already, in my consciousness, I can make the correct choices on my path, which often helps me be in the correct place to help others. In this way I can be more of service, which is my life's purpose.

My philosophy of life has changed into a study of non-judgment. I have told you how important the life review was for me in this, and how it continues to be significant as a tool for growth. Every one of us can create his or her own life review by reviewing the day. When reviewing the day, remember to do it without judgment and be gentle. Think about what happened today: *"Well, I was a little abrupt when I didn't receive the service I requested."* Say: *"I can do better next time, I still love myself."* Do not judge—there is no judgment in a life review or a day review. A review is a learning and evolving technique that benefits the soul.

Once you can do a review on a daily basis, the next goal is to work toward a moment-to-moment review. If you do the review first as a discipline eventually you will observe it evolving into a habit and the Natural Way, which brings you closer to Buddhist mindfulness. In review you begin to see your path through the synchronicities in your life. These synchronicities become more frequent and you recognize them quicker. The most useful part of a review is figuring out what you can learn from it. *"How has it helped me grow?"* The review also helps you to recognize the cycles in your life. You'll know when it's the beginning of one cycle and the ending of another. Ask: *"What is this cycle I'm in? Why the shift? "There's something happening I don't understand, but help me get a handle on it."* A daily review will help smooth out transition periods.

We begin to know ourselves and understand others without getting caught up in the stage show. We learn to love beyond the drama that surrounds us. As you grow with your practice remember the basics of Acceptance, Tolerance, Truth, and respect our environment. Go through the day without judgment, and start using mindfulness. We near-death experiencers are reminded daily of our time in the Light. We try to apply the lessons we learned there to what we are experiencing now. *"You have a purpose"* rings in my ears many times each day and keeps me mindful of my promise to communicate and share Spirit with others. In this way I continue my quiet ministry.

Recently I reevaluated where I am in my life's path. I am thrilled with my new mission statement: *"Sow helpful seeds imbued with loving Light to all that interact in my life's path."* Sowing seeds brings responsibility, so as I share I am mindful about how my love affects others. Keeping my heart open, the energy I communicate is always felt but not always understood. So I stay mindful of the power inherent in our interconnectedness, especially when passions are at their peak. I just have to remember my life review and how my passions created some of the greatest ripples, positive and negative.

I believe that, as a vehicle of intention, prayer can affect the most positive actions for the greater good of all. I believe prayer can create miracles, and that I am a living example of prayer's power. The hundreds who prayed for me to return to health during my bout with cancer is my confirmation. We maintain a healing altar in our home and use it regularly to pray for friends and family.

Finally, I would like to say that all the experiences we have in this life are important. It is only our perceptions that label experiences good or bad. Experiences are what make us grow. They make our spirit grow. How we deal with responsibilities, experiences and opportunities are of great consequence. Because we are all from the Light, we don't have to go searching for Spirit. Spirit is within us all, and all we have to do is to be mindful and listen. When we are able to do that, we get the clarity and understanding of where we need to be, so that each of us may live our lives just a little bit better.

Appendix A

❀ Books and Publications About NDEs And Spiritually Transformative Experiences ❀

Attwater, PMH, *Beyond the Light: What Isn't Being Said about Near-Death Experiences,* Transpersonal Publishing (September 23, 2009)
— *Coming Back to Life: Examining the After-Effects of the Near-Death Experience,* Transpersonal Publishing; Revised Edition edition (May 15, 2008)
— *Future Memory,* Hampton Roads Pub Co; 1 edition (January 1, 1999)
— *The Big Book of Near-Death Experiences,* Hampton Roads Pub Co (October 19, 2007)
— *The New Children and Near-Death Experiences,* Bear & Company (December 31, 2003)
— *We Live Forever: The Real Truth About Death,* A.R.E. Press (Association of Research & Enlightenment (June 2004)

Baumann, T. Lee, *The Akashic Light: Religion's Common Thread,* A. R. E. Press (June 1, 2006)

Brinkley, Dannion, with Paul Perry, *Saved by the Light: The True Story of a Man Who Died Twice and the Profound Revelations He Received,* HarperOne; Reprint edition (November 25, 2008)

Callanan, Maggie, and Patricia Kelly, *Final Gifts: Understanding the Special Awareness, Needs, and Communications of the Dying,* Bantam; (February 3, 1997)

Campbell, Joseph, and Bill Moyers, *The Power of Myth,* Anchor (June 1, 1991)

Campbell, Joseph, and Phil Cousineau, *The Hero's Journey: Joseph Campbell on His Life and Work,* New World Library; 3rd edition (August 27, 2003)

Chesbro, Rev. Daniel, *The Order of Melchizedek: Love, Willing Service, & Fulfillment,* Findhorn Press (October 1, 2010)

Cohhen, Tammy, *The Day I Died: Remarkable True Stories of Near-Death Experience*, John Blake (May 1, 2006)

Danison, Nanci L., Backwards: Returning to Our Source for Answers, A.P. Lee & Co.; (October 15, 2007)

Dougherty, Ned, *Fast Lane to Heaven: A Life-After-Death Journey*, Hampton Roads Pub Co (October 1, 2002)

Eadie, Betty, *Embraced by the Light*, Bantam (October 29, 2002)

Elder, Paul, *Eyes Of An Angel: Soul Travel, Spirit Guides, Soul Mates, And The Reality Of Love*, Hampton Roads Pub Co (April 30, 2005)

Guggenheim, Bill, and Judy Guggenheim, *Hello from Heaven: A New Field of Research-After-Death Communication Confirms That Life and Love Are Eternal*, Bantam (March 3, 1997)

Hemingway, Annamaria, *Practicing Conscious Living and Dying: Stories of the Eternal Continuum of Consciousness*, O Books (December 20, 2007)

Holden, Janice, Bruce Greyson, and Debbie James, *The Handbook of Near-Death Experiences: Thirty Years of Investigation,* Praeger (June 22, 2009)

Jorgensen, Rene, *Awakening after Life: A Firsthand Guide through Death into the Purpose of Life*, BookSurge Publishing (May 31, 2007)
— *The Light Behind God: What Religion Can Learn From Near Death Experiences*, CreateSpace (January 3, 2010)

Kircher, Pamela M., *Love is the Link: A Hospice Doctor Shares Her Experience of Near Death and Dying,* Larson Publications (November 25, 1995)

Kelly, Edward and Emily Williams Kelly & Bruce Greyson, *Irreducible Mind: Toward a Psychology for the 21st Century*, Rowman & Littlefield Publishers, Inc. (November 16, 2009)

Kubler-Ross, Elisabeth, *On Death and Dying*, Scribner (July 2, 1997)

Lerma, John, *Into the Light: Real Life Stories About Angelic Visits, Visions of the Afterlife, and Other Pre-Death Experiences*, New Page Books (November 30, 2007)

Long, Jeffery, **with Paul Perry**, *Evidence of the Afterlife: The Science of Near-Death Experiences*, HarperOne; (January 4, 2011)

Lucas, Catherine G., *In Case of Spiritual Emergency: Moving Successfully Through Your Awakening*, Findhorn Press (August 1, 2011)

McTaggart, Lynne, *The Intention Experiment: Using Your Thoughts to Change Your Life and the World*, Free Press (February 5, 2008)

Moody Raymond, *Life After Life: The Investigation of a Phenomenon-Survival of Bodily Death*, HarperOne (March 6, 2001)

Morse, Melvin, *Closer to the Light: Learning from Children's Near-Death Experiences*, Ivy Books (July 30, 1991)
— *Where God Lives: The Science of the Paranormal and How Our Brains are Linked to the Universe*, HarperOne (September 4, 2001)

O'Brien, Frances, *A Benevolent Virus*, O Books (November 16, 2010)

Pagels, Elain, The Gnostic Gospels, Vintage (September 19, 1989)

Parnia, Sam, *What Happens When We Die?: A Groundbreaking Study into the Nature of Life and Death, Hay House* (February 1, 2007)

Radin, Dean, *Entangled Minds: Extrasensory Experiences in a Quantum Reality*, Paraview Pocket Books (April 25, 2006)

Ring, Kenneth, and Evelyn Elsaesser Valarino, *Lessons from the Light: What We Can Learn from the Near-death Experience*, Moment Point Press; (September 1, 2006)
— *Mindsight: Near-Death and Out-of-Body Experiences in the Blind*, IUniverse; (March 14, 2008)

Ritchie, George G., and Elizabeth Sherrill, *Return from Tomorrow*, Chosen; Anv edition (September 1, 2007)

Sabom, Michael B., *Light and Death: one Doctor's Fascinating Account of Near-Death Experiences*, Zondervan (November 1, 1998)

Sawyer, Tom, and Sidney Saylor Farr, *What Tom Sawyer Learned from Dying*, Hampton Roads Publishing Co. (April 1993) - Out of Print

Schlitz, Marilyn Mandala , Cassandra Vieten and Tina Amorok, *Living Deeply: The Art and Science of Transformation in Everyday Life*, Noetic Book / New Harbinger Publications (January 3, 2008)

Schwartz, Gary E., William Simon, *The Afterlife Experiments: Breakthrough Scientific Evidence of Life After Death*, Atria (March 18, 2003)

Schwartz, Robert, *Your Soul's Plan: Discovering the Real Meaning of the Life You Planned Before You Were Born*, Frog Books (March 24, 2009)

Sharp, Kimberly Clark, *AFTER THE LIGHT: What I Discovered on the Other Side of Life That Can Change Your World*, IUniverse (June 12, 2003)

Shockey, Peter and Stowe Shockey, *Journey of Light: Stories of Dawn After Darkness*, Doubleday (February 20, 2007)

Sogyal Rinpoche, Patrick D. Gaffney and Andrew Harvey, The Tibetan Book of Living and Dying: The Spiritual Classic & International Bestseller, HarperOne; Revised edition (March 17, 1994)

Storm, Howard, *My Descent Into Death: A Second Chance at Life*, Harmony; First Edition (February 15, 2005)

Tolle, Eckhart, *A New Earth: Awakening to Your Life's Purpose*, Penguin (January 30, 2008)
— *The Power of Now: A Guide to Spiritual Enlightenment*, New World Library (September 29, 2004)

Twyman, James F., *The Art of Spiritual Peacemaking*, Findhorn Press (April 1, 2006)

Van Lommel, Pim, *Consciousness Beyond Life: The Science of the Near-Death Experience*, HarperOne (June 8, 2010)

Whitfield, Barbara Harris, *The Natural Soul*, Muse House Press/Pennington (January 1, 2010)

Appendix B

❀ Websites About NDEs And Spiritually Transformative Experiences ❀

David Bennett, (Author / Speaker / Experiencer)
www.VoyageofPurpose.com Official (Website for extra content and help in living with purpose.)
www.DharmaTalks.com Personal site with news and insights.

Cindy Griffith-Bennett, (Psychic / Author / Teacher)
www.PsychicSupport.com

After-Death Communication,—Hello from Heaven! by Bill and Judy Guggenheim, (Authors / Researcher) www.after-death.com

American Center for the Integration of Spiritually Transformative Experiences, (Creating programs that facilitate integration for experiencers.)
www.aciste.org

P.M.H Atwater, (Author / Researcher / Experiencer)
www.pmhatwater.com

Institute of HeartMath, (Research / Education / Membership Organization dedicated to helping people establish heart-based living and global coherence.)
www.heartmath.org

Institute of Noetic Sciences, (IONS) (Research / Education / Membership Organization whose mission is supporting individual and collective transformation through consciousness research)
www.noetic.org

International Association for Near-Death Studies, Inc. (IANDS) (Research / Education / Support / Membership Organization / Reliable information about near-death experiences, and local groups)
www.iands.org

Rene Jorgensen, (Video Interviews of Experiencers)
www.youtube.com/user/LightBehindGod

Elisabeth Kubler-Ross Foundation, (Information about end-of-life care, hospice, the Five Stages of Grief and Palliative Care)
www.ekrfoundation.org

Near-Death Experience Research Foundation, (Over 2500 full-text published NDE accounts)
www.nderf.org

Near-Death Experiencers, (Spiritual Retreat for Near-Death Experiencers)
www.neardeathexperiencers.org

Near-Death Experiences and the Afterlife, by Kevin Williams (variety of NDE Resources)
www.near-death.com

Open Directory—Near-Death Experiences, (variety)
www.dmoz.org/Society/Death/Near_Death_Experiences

Out of Body Experience Research Foundation, Jody & Dr. Jeffery Long (spiritually transformative events, consciousness studies, extensive information and research)
www.oberf.org

Bill Taylor (Experiencer videos on YouTube)
www.youtube.com/user/billsvideos123

Appendix C

❀ Blogs and Social Networks About NDEs And Spiritually Transformative Experiences ❀

David Bennett, (Author / Speaker / Experiencer)
www.dharmatalks.wordpress.com (blog)
www.twitter.com/#!/DharmaTalks (twitter)
DharmaTalks on Facebook

Cindy Griffith-Bennett, (Psychic / Author / Teacher)
Cindy Griffiths—Giving Back Page on Facebook

ACISTE Experiencer Forum (American Center for the Integration of Spiritually Transformative Experiences Social Network)
www.aciste.ning.com

P.M.H Atwater, (Author / Researcher / Experiencer)
www.pmhatwater.blogspot.com (blog)

NDE-Space (Near-Death Experience Social Network)
www.ndespace.org

NHNE Near-Death Experience Network, (Social Network, Exploring all aspects of the near-death experience.)
www.nhneneardeath.ning.com

❀ ENDNOTES ❀

Acknowledgements
Saint Ambrose (340-397 AD), De Spiritu Sancto

Chapter One

Gautama Buddha, Dhammapada, Ch.165 (4th or 5th century)
Eckhart Tolle, from *A New Earth* by Eckhart Tolle, copyright © 2005 by Eckhart Tolle. Used by permission of Dutton, a division of Penguin Group (USA) Inc. pp. 194 -195
1.1 Elisabeth Kubler-Ross, from the Elisabeth Kubler-Ross Foundation at http://www.elisabethkublerross.com/
1.2 Leo Tolstoy, *What Men Live By and Other Tales* translated by L. and A. Maude (Boston: The Stratford Company Publishers, 1918) Ch. XII p. 33
1.3 Ralph Waldo Emerson, *Works of Ralph Waldo Emerson* (London: George Routledge and Sons, 1897) p. 428

Chapter Two

Chandogya Upanishad, *The story of Shvetaketu* Ch. VI 10.1-10.2
2.1 Edgar Cayce, *The Edgar Cayce Companion*, by B. Ernest Frejer, (Virginia Beach, Virginia: A.R.E. Press, 1995) p. 59. Edgar Cayce Readings © 1971, 1993-2005 by the Edgar Cayce Foundation. All Rights Reserved.
2.2 Dionysius the Areopagite, *On the Divine Names*, c. 500
2.3 Henry David Thoreau, *Life Without Principle* The Atlantic Monthly, (October 1863)
2.4 Gautama Buddha, *Dhammapada,* (4th or 5th century)
2.5 Meister Eckhart, *Meister Eckhart's Sermons* Sanctification translated into English by Claud Field (1909) Sermon VI :

2.6 Sir Walter Scott, *Sir Walter Scott, Waverley novels*: Volume 24 (Boston, MA: Samuel H. Parker, 1831) p.197

Chapter Three

Schaff, Philip, *The Confessions and Letters of St. Augustine* (Grand Rapids: WM. B. Eeerdmans Publishing, 1886) Ch.VIII
3.1 Mother Teresa, from the book *No Greater Love*. Copyright © 1997, 2001 by New World Library, p.66. Reprinted with permission of New World Library, Novato, CA. www.newworldlibrary.com.
3.2 Diamond Sutra or Prajna-paramita, translated by William Gemmell (London: Kegan Paul, Trench, Trubner & Co., 1913)
3.3 Marcus Aurelius, *Discourses of Epictetus*, translated by George Long (New York, D.Appleton & Co., 1900) p.29
3.4 Jalāl ad-Dīn Mu'ammad Rūmī, Divan-e Shams-e Tabrizi, Quatrain 1161 (around 1250)
3.5 Augustine of Hippo, *On True Religions* (390 AD)
3.6 Kalidas, Sanskrit dramatist (4th or 5th century)
3.7 Kahlil Gibran, *The Prophet* (1923) p. 13
Lao-tzu, *Tao Te Ching* translated by J. Legge v. 50 (1891)

Chapter Four

Srimad Bhagavad Gita, Translated by Swami Paramananda (Boston, Mass: The Vedanta Center, 1913) p. 14
4.1 Sri Aurobindo, *Arya Ch. 1, Indian Spirituality and Life* (August 1919)
4.2 Gautama Buddha, *The Dhammapada*, Translator: F. Max Müller (Oxford: the Clarendon Press, 1881) Ch. 1
Yolaine Stout, Linda Jacquin, and PMH Atwater, *Six Major Challenges faced by Near-Death Experiencers*, IANDS, Journal of Near-Death Studies, Vol 25, Number1, (Fall 2006)
4.3 Friedrich Wilhelm Nietzsche, Human, *All too Human* (1878) II.358
4.4 Mother Teresa, from the book *No Greater Love*. Copyright © 1997, 2001 by New World Library p. 25. Reprinted with permission of New World Library, Novato, CA. www.newworldlibrary.com.

Chapter Five

Brihadaranyaka Upanishad, *The Path to Immortality*, Ch. II 4.12

5.1 Plato, Dialogues of Plato, Translated by B. Jowett (1871) p. 414

5.2 Maulana Jalalu-'d-din Muhammad Rumi, *The Masnavi I Ma'navi of Rumi: Complete*, translated by E.H. Whinfeild (1898) p. 62

5.3 Maulana Jalalu-'d-din Muhammad Rumi, *The Masnavi I Ma'navi of Rumi: Complete*, translated by E.H. Whinfeild (1898) p. 4

5.4 Brihad-Aranyaka Upanishads 3.2.13, *The Thirteen Principle Upanishads (England: Oxford University Press, 1921)* p. 110

Chapter Six

Mohandas Karamchand Gandhi, *(from an address to members of a college at Colombo)* Charles F. Andrews, Mahatma Gandhi's Ideas (1931) pp.92-97

6.1 Socrates, quoted by Xenophon, Memorabilia I. 4.18

6.2 Edgar Cayce, *The Edgar Cayce Companion*, by B. Ernest Frejer, (Virginia Beach, Virginia: A.R.E. Press, 1995) p. 344. *Edgar Cayce Readings* © 1971, 1993-2005 by the Edgar Cayce Foundation. All Rights Reserved.

6.3 Ralph Waldo Emerson, American philosopher, essayist, and poet (1803—1882)

6.4 Friedrich Nietzsche, Beyond Good and Evil, Aphorism v. 146 (1886)

Chapter Seven

Arthur Christopher Benson, *From a College Window*, (1906) English essayist, poet, and author.

7.2 Sri Aurobindo, from a letter Sri Aurobindo wrote in Bengali to his wife, Mrinalini Devi. (1872—1905)

7.3 Victor Hugo, *William Shakespeare*, (1864)

7.4 Adi Shankara, *Bhaja Govindam*, a Hindu philosopher (788—820 CE) Hindu devotional composition in Sanskrit.

Chapter Eight

Elisabeth Kubler-Ross, from the Elisabeth Kubler-Ross Foundation at http://www.elisabethkublerross.com/

8.1 The Bhagavad Gita, v. 2-14 (between the 5th and 2nd century BCE)

8.2 Charles Dickens, *The Chimes*, (1844)

8.3 Edgar Cayce, *The Edgar Cayce Companion,* by B. Ernest Frejer, (Virginia Beach, Virginia: A.R.E. Press 1995) p. 258 Edgar Cayce Readings © 1971, 1993-2005 by the Edgar Cayce Foundation. All Rights Reserved

8.4 William Ralph Inge, *Survival and Immortality* (1919)

Chapter Nine

Maulana Jalalu-'d-din Muhammad Rumi, The Masnavi I Ma'navi of Rumi: Complete, translated by E.H. Whinfeild (1898) pp. 234-235
9.1 John Milton, an English poet (1608—1674)
9.2 Pope St. Gregory the Great, Morals on the book of Job, (584 AD)

Chapter Ten

Epictetus, *Golden Sayings of Epictetus* (37), translated by Hastings Crossley (London: Macmillan and Co., 1912) pp. 30 - 31
Sherry Hansen Steiger & Brad Steiger, *Christmas Miracles: Inspirational stories of True Holiday Magic,* (Avon, MA: Adams Media Corp, 2001)

Chapter Eleven

Rabindranath Tagore, *The Gardener v.85* (NewYork: the Macmillan Co., 1915) p. 146
11.1 Thomas Carlyle, *On Heroes and Hero Worship, Lecture V* (London: Chapman and Hall, 1840) p.40
11.2 Theodore Chickering Williams, *The Voyage of Life, Bartlett's Familiar Quotations,* 10th ed. (1919)
11.3 Chandogya Upanishad, *Narada's Education* Ch. VII 24.1

Chapter Twelve

Rabindranath Tagore, Sādhanā : *The Realization of Life* (New York: The Macmillan Co., 1916) p.116
12.1 Joseph Campbell, *The Joseph Campbell Companion: Reflections on the Art of Living* p. 22, 63: copyright © 1991; reprinted by permission of Joseph Campbell Foundation (jcf.org).
12.3 Cicero, De Finibus, (c50 BCE)
Yolaine M. Stout, Linda A. Jacquin and P.M.H. Atwater, *Six Major Challenges Faced by Near-Death Experiencers* (Durham NC: IANDS Journal of Near-Death Studies, 2006) Vol. 25, #1
12.4 Ramakrishna, *The Gospel of Sri Ramakrishna vol. 1* translated by Swami Nikhilananda (New York: Ramakrishna-Vivekananda Center, January 1942) p.818

12.5 Lyev Nikolayevich Tolstoy, *Tolstoy's diaries vol 2*, edited and translated by R. F. Christian. (London: Athlone Press,) p. 512

12.6 Epictetus, *The Enchiridion v.15*, translated by George Long (1877)

Life-Changing Books

For a complete catalogue,
please contact:

Findhorn Press
117–121 High Street
Forres IV36 1AB
Scotland, UK

t +44-(0)1309-690582
f +44-(0)131-777-2711
e info@findhornpress.com

or consult our catalogue online
(with secure order facility) on
www.findhornpress.com

For information on the Findhorn Foundation:
www.findhorn.org